Facetiae Cantabrigienses
by Richard Gooch

Address:
HardPress
8345 NW 66TH ST #2561
MIAMI FL 33166-2626
USA
Email: info@hardpress.net

Facetiae cantabrigienses

Richard Gooch

PROFESSOR PORSON.

Published by W. COLE 10. Newgate Str

FACETIÆ CANTABRIGIENSES:

CONSISTING OF

ANECDOTES,

SMART SAYINGS, SATIRICS, RETORTS, &c. &c.

BY OR RELATING TO

Celebrated Cantabs.

Τὸν λόγον σου θαυμάσας ἔχω.—PLATO.

DEDICATED TO THE STUDENTS OF LINCOLN'S INN,

BY SOCIUS.

LONDON:

PRINTED FOR WILLIAM COLE, NEWGATE STREET.

1825.

Davidson and Son,
rle's Place, London.

PREFACE.

I HAVE often, during my residence in Cambridge, regretted that many very facetious and richly-spiced anecdotes, and smart sayings, should only be handed round the University by *tradition;* and not only are they entirely lost to the world, but many—I believe I may add, a very great number—of the members of the University are almost ignorant of their existence. Hence I resolved to compile the

Facetiae Cantabrigienses;

And I trust I shall be, if not commended, at least pardoned, for so doing. The eye of the reader will sometimes come in contact with an anecdote which is already familiar to him: this he will perhaps forgive; as my aim is, not only to make him acquainted with strangers, but also to collect the lost sheep, which are to be found scattered up and down, in various publications, and, like the Jews, have no particular resting-place.

PREFACE.

Being myself a mortal enemy to *long prefaces*, I shall make my bow by observing—that most men are occasionally troubled with *ennui*, or, as it is sometimes denominated—

"THE BLUE DEVILS;"

and I know of no better remedy for such maladies, than that afforded by a perusal of the

FACETIOUS.

CONTENTS.

CONTENTS.

CONTENTS.

CAMBRIDGE PARTIES, BY TWO DISTINGUISHED CANTABS:

Facetiæ Cantabrigienses.

UTOPIA.

A Satire, in imitation of a Mathematical Examination Paper; said to be written by a Gentleman of Sidney Sussex College, A.D. 1816.

1.—FIND the *actual value* of 0, and from thence explain the general expression of a man sending a *circular letter to his creditors*.

2.—Construct a *craniometer* on the principle of the *hydrometer*, pointing out the uses to which such an instrument will be applicable.

3.—An orifice is cut reaching from the surface to the centre of the ⊕ ; in what time will a *cub* of given magnitude descend with the velocity in a chase of a given number of miles?

4.—Find the periodic time of the *honey-moon*, and determine, in general, when the *horns* are first apparent.

5.—The successive ascents of wind in the stomach are in *musical progression* : required, a proof.

6.—Where must an eye be placed to see distinctly the books missing from the University Library, the fountain of the Nile, and the author of these problems ?

7.—Given that a man can stand twenty-four hours on wo legs; show that the same man can stand twelve ours on one.

8.—Investigate an expression for the law of the *centri-ugal force* of *modern extempore discourses.*

9.—To determine the least possible quantity of *mate-·ial* out of which the modern dress of a fashionable fe-nale can be constructed.

10.—Prove all the roots of *radical reform* to be either *rrational* or *impossible.*

11.—Given the three sides of a steel triangle im-nersed in *sulphuric acid*: required, a solution of the ·riangle.

12.—Compare the eccentricities of Lord Stanhope, :he comet of 1811, and Sir Frederick Flood?

13.—Reconcile Hoyle and Euclid, the latter of whom lefines a point to be without magnitude, the former to equal five.

14.—Sum your rental to N terms by the method of increments, your debts *ad infinitum* by the differential method.

15.—Find practically the nature and length of a *lu-nar caustic.*

16.—Seven funipendulous bodies are suspended from different points in a common system at the *Old Bailey*: to find the centre of oscillation.

17.—Required to express the *function* of a sinecure.

18.—To compare the dimensions of the base of the Hottentot Venus, and that of the broad-bottomed admi-nistration.

18.—The curve is an old woman bent double very nearly; determine the point of *contrary* flexure, and find, if possible, the *latus rectum.*

20.—Find the whole area of the *wooden* spoon, and compare that of the *Holy Land* with the area of that part of it generally called *Clapham Common*.

21.—Investigate the magnifying power of the eye of the Baron Munchausen, and show that any straight line placed before it will form a *conic section*, no other than the *common hyperbola*.

22.—Construct a theorem, by the assistance of which the periodic time of *status pupillaris* may be extended to any number of *terms*.

23.—In the general equation (Algebra, Part Second), show that the probable reason why Wood invariably uses p and q, in preference to the other letters of the *alphabet*, may be deduced from the general expression, *mind your P's and Q's.*

24.—Given a *Berkshire* pig, a *Johnian* pig, and a pig of *lead;* to find their respective *densities.*

PORSON'S VISIT TO THE CONTINENT.

Soon after the late Professor Porson returned from a visit to the Continent, at a party where he happened to be present, a gentleman solicited a sketch of his journey. Porson immediately gave the following extemporaneous one :—

" I went to Frankfort and got drunk
With that most learned professor, Brunck ;
I went to Worts and got more drunken
With that more learned professor, Ruhnken."

" I'M ASLEEP."

A Cantab being out of ready cash, went in haste to a fellow-student to borrow, who happened to be in bed at the time. Shaking him, the Cantab demanded,—" *Are you asleep?*"—" *Why?*" says the student. " *Because,*" replied the other, " *I want to borrow half-a-crown.*—" *Then,*" answered the student, " *I'm asleep.*"

JOHN BO-PEEP.

Tom Randolph, who was then a student in Cambridge, having staid in London so long that he might truly be said to have had a *parley with his empty purse,* was resolved to see Ben Jonson with his associates, who, as he heard, at a set time, kept a club together at the Devil Tavern, near Temple Bar. Accordingly he went thither at the specified time; but, being unknown to them, and wanting money, which, to a spirit like Tom's, was the most daunting thing in the world, he peeped into the room where they were, and was espied by Ben Jonson, who, seeing him in a scholar's thread-bare habit, cried out, " *John Bo-peep, come in !*" which accordingly he did. They immediately began to rhyme upon the meanness of his clothes, asking him if he could not make a verse, and, withal, to call for his quart of sack. There being but four of them, he immediately replied—

I John Bo-peep,
To you four sheep,
With each one his good fleece ;

If that you are willing.
To give me five shilling,—
'Tis fifteen pence a-piece.

" By Jesus," exclaimed Ben Jonson (his usual oath),
" I believe this is my son Randolph ;" which being
made known to them, he was kindly entertained in
their company, and Ben Jonson ever after called him
his son.

" YOU'LL GET THERE BEFORE I CAN TELL YOU."

Mr. Neville, formerly a fellow of Jesus College, was
greatly respected for his peaceable and inoffensive manners, but distinguished by many innocent singularities,
uncommon shyness, and stammering of speech. Dr.
Caryl has observed, " that when he used *bad* words he
could talk fluently." A sudden address from a stranger
would disconcert him beyond measure. In one of his
solitary rambles, a countryman met him, and inquired
the road. " Tu—u—rn," says Neville, " to—to—to—"
and so on for a minute or two ; at last he burst out,
" *Damn it, man ! you'll get there before I can tell you!*"

DR. JOHN HEY,

When he kept a public *act* in the schools at the University of Cambridge, towards the conclusion of the
disputation, availed himself of the arguments of Dr.
Beattie and others of the *Scotch school.* Dr. Watson,

who was then Regius Professor of Divinity, and abundantly well read in ancient theology, burst forth with the following *apophthegma*, " *Quid hi Scotti sentient, nescio ; sed quæ sentire debent, benè scio !*"

LOAVES AND FISHES.

Soon after Mr. Pitt became *Premier*, he happened to be in Cambridge at the Commencement, when the late Dr. Paley, author of Moral Philosophy, &c. was appointed to preach the sermon before the heads and the members of the different colleges, in the University church. Mr. Pitt, who was then a young man, was one of the congregation. Many of the members of the University, from the official situation he had obtained, and his connection with them, being their representative in Parliament, anticipated church preferment through his interest. On this occasion Dr. Paley, remarkable for his independent spirit, chose the following pointed text :—

" There is a lad here, which hath *five barley loaves* and *two small fishes :* but what are they among so many ?"

JOHN, vi. 9.

A SINE.

A student, at an examination in Trinity College, being required to define a *Sine*, gave the following laconic answer :—" An evil and adulterous generation seek for a *Sine*, but they shall not find one, except that of the prophet Jonah."

ST. JOHN'S HEAD ON A CHARGER.

A fellow of St. John's College walking with a friend, who was a stranger in Cambridge, by chance met the master of his college, Dr. Wood, on horseback; and, on his friend asking who the gentleman on horseback was, he facetiously replied, "*It is St. John's head on a charger.*"

BISHOP BLAIZE.

An honest publican, who was his neighbour, in order to testify his respect for the late Bishop Watson, took down his long-established sign of Bishop Blaize, and substituted for it the head of Dr. Watson. A wicked wag of the University, who was afterwards Bishop of Bristol, wrote the following epigram on the occasion:

" Two of a trade can ne'er agree,
    No proverb e'er was juster;
They've ta'en down Bishop Blaize, do you see,
    And put up Bishop Bluster."

THE CAUSEWAY.

Dr. Harvey, of Trinity Hall, made a causeway for about three miles from Cambridge towards Newmarket, and one morning, as he was overlooking the workmen, a certain nobleman, who suspected the doctor's inclinations to popery, said to him, " I suppose, doctor, you imagine this the highway to heaven."—" No, no,

THE METAMORPHOSIS.

A party of Cantabs one day, walking along a street in Cambridge, espied an ass tied to a door, and being in want of an object wherewith to kill a little time, they resolved to play *bumpkin* a trick, who, having disposed of his wares, was enjoying his pipe and his pint within doors. The Cantabs were not long at a loss what to be at, one of them proposing that the *panniers* should be put upon his back, and the bridle on his head, whilst the rest led the *ass* astray. In this condition stood the scholar, when bumpkin, who had by this time finished his pipe and pint, came to the door; all amazement at what he saw, he stood gaping for a minute or two, when the Cantab thus addressed him :—"You must know, Sir, that I quarrelled with my father about seven years since, and, for my disobedience, I was changed into the degrading shape of an *ass*, to endure every hardship for that space of time; which being now expired, you are bound to set me at liberty." Bumpkin, believing the tale, took off the panniers and bridle, and set the scholar at large. A few days after, Bumpkin went to a neighbouring *country fair* to purchase another *ass*, in lieu of the one he had lost; and, after viewing different beasts, to his no small surprise, his old identical ass was offered to him; which, on seeing its master, brayed most piteously in token of recognition; but Hodge, nothing moved thereat, passed on to another, exclaiming—"So you have quarrelled with your father again, have you? But dang me if I'll have you again!"

"I DIDN'T GET IT."

A certain doctor, head of a college, stood candidate for a professorship which happened to be vacant at the same time his lady was delivered of a fine boy. A friend called on the doctor about the time the professorship was decided, and for which he was one of the unsuccessful candidates, to congratulate him on the birth of his son; and accordingly, in the usual phrase, "wished him joy." The doctor being rather deaf, and mistaking his meaning, replied rather smartly, "*I didn't get it;—I didn't get it.*"

ST. PETER A BACHELOR.

In the list of benefactors to Peter-House is Lady Mary Ramsay, who is reported to have offered a very large property, nearly equal to a new foundation to this college, on condition that the name should be changed to *Peter and Mary's*; but she was thwarted in her intention by Dr. Soame, then master. "Peter," said the crabbed humourist, "has been too long a *bachelor* to think of a female companion in his old days."

THE NIGHTCAP.

The Rev. George Harvest, fellow of Magdalen College, Cambridge, with a good heart possessed many oddities. One night, seated amidst all the pageantry of politeness with Lady O— and the family, in the front box of a London theatre, poor Harvest, on pulling out his handkerchief, brought with it an old *greasy nightcap*, which fell into the pit. "Who owns this?" cries a gentleman below, elevating the trophy. at the same time on the point of his cane; "Who owns this?" The unaffected Harvest, little considering the delicate sensations of his friends, and overjoyed at the recovery of this valuable chattle, eagerly darts out his hand, seizes the cap, and in the action cries out, "It is mine!" The party were utterly disconcerted at the circumstance, and blushed for their companion, who rather expected their congratulations at the recovery of his property.

A CUNNING SHAVER.

It is sufficiently notorious that Porson was not remarkably attentive to the decorating of his person; indeed he was at times disagreeably negligent. On one occasion he went to visit a friend, where a gentleman, who did not know Porson, was anxiously expecting a barber. On Porson's entering the library where he was sitting, the gentleman started up, and hastily exclaimed, " Are you the barber?"—" *No, Sir*," answered Porson; " *but I am a cunning shaver, much at your service.*"

ARCHBISHOP HERRING IN PICKLE.

Herring, afterwards archbishop, slipt down a bank, and fell into the mud in a ditch near St. John's College. A wag, passing by at the time, exclaimed, "There, Herring, you are in a fine pickle now!" A Johnian, to which college the immemorial privilege of punning had been conceded in the Spectator's time, and who had consequently a disposition to be pleased with *puns*, went home laughing most immoderately all the way at the joke. Some of his fellow-collegians inquiring the cause of his merriment: " I never heard," said he, " a better thing in my life. Herring, of Jesus, fell into the ditch in the piece, and an acquaintance said, as he lay sprawling, ' There, Herring! you are in a fine *condition* now!' "—" Well," said his companions, " where is the wit of it, pray?"— " Nay," he said, " I am sure it was a good thing when I heard it."

" DO YOU KNOW WHO I AM ?"

It has been a custom in the University, from time immemorial, to *cap* the Vice-Chancellor. A student meeting Dr. ——, Master of Clare Hall, when he held that office, and omitting to pay him the accustomed compliment, the doctor, conceiving it to be an insult to his dignity, stopped the student, exclaiming, at the same time, " Do you know who I am, Sir?" The student, taking his glass, coolly eyed the doctor from head to foot, answering, " Upon my word, Sir, I have not that pleasure."—" Sir," said the doctor, " I am the Vice-Chancellor."—" Indeed!" said the student: at the same instant *capping* the doctor, he walked on.

TREASON.

It is related of the two admirable wits, *Beaumont* and *Fletcher*, that, meeting once in a tavern to contrive the rude draught of a tragedy, Fletcher undertook to *kill the king* therein ; whose words being overheard by a *listener*, ne was accused of *high treason*; but the mistake soon appearing, that the plot was only against a *dramatical* and *scenical king*, it passed off in merriment.

PARLIAMENTARY CASE.

Bishop Andrews, who was master and a great benefactor of Pembroke Hall, was one day at court with Walter the poet and others. While King James was at dinner, attended by Andrews, Bishop of Winchester, and Neale, Bishop of Durham, his Majesty said to the prelates,—" My Lords, cannot I take my subjects' *money* when I want it, without all this formality in Parliament?" Bishop Neale quickly replied,—" God forbid, Sir, but you should : you are the breath of our nostrils." On which the king said to the Bishop of Winchester,— " Well, my Lord, and what say you ?"—" Sir," replied Andrews, " I have no skill to judge of Parliamentary cases."—" Come, come," answered his Majesty, " no put-offs, my Lord; answer me presently."—" Then, Sir," said Andrews, " I think it lawful for you to take my brother Neale's money, for he offers it."

SALUTING A DOG WITH HIS OWN LATIN.

During the time that Mr. F. was Moderator, a dog one day happened, not being initiated in the etiquette necessary to be observed, to stray into the schools at Cambridge, when a student was keeping an act. It fell to the turn of Mr. F. to preside that day, and the moment the poor dog made his entré, Mr. F. thundered out the following apophthegma—" *Verte canem ex !*"

AS GREAT A ROGUE AS HIMSELF.

Jemmy Gordon, a well-known character in Cambridge, once went to the late Bishop of Bristol, of facetious memory, who was then Master of Trinity College, to request that he would give him *half-a-crown*. " So I will," replied the bishop, " if you can find me as great a rogue as yourself." Jemmy Gordon, nothing doubting but he should be able to accommodate the bishop, and obtain the desired half-crown, went immediately to Mr. B——, who was at that time one of the Esquire Bedells of the university, and told him the bishop wanted to speak with him. Mr. B——, not suspecting Jemmy's trick, went directly to the bishop, followed, unperceived, by Jemmy Gordon ; and, on entering his presence, he desired " to know his lordship's pleasure ?" The bishop, to his surprise, said he had not sent for him ! But Jemmy Gordon, who was nigh at hand, informed his lordship, " that he told him he would give him half-a-crown if he could find as great a rogue as himself, and, having produced Mr. B——, he claimed the promised reward." The bishop was so well pleased with the joke, that he gave Jemmy the half-crown.

PRINCE'S METAL.

When the Prince of Orange, afterwards William the Third, came over to this country, five of the seven bishops who were sent to the Tower declared for his highness ; but the other two would not come into the measures. Upon which *Dryden* . said, " that the seven

golden candlesticks were sent to be assayed in the
Tower, and five of them proved *prince's metal.*"

PALEY,

Soon after he had completed his fifteenth year, went
to Cambridge, accompanied by his father, to be admitted a sizar of Christ College; to which society his
father had belonged before him. He performed this
journey on horseback, and used often thus humorously
to describe the disasters which befel him on the road:
—" I was never a good horseman, and, when I followed
my father on a pony of my own, on my first journey to
Cambridge, I fell off seven times. I was lighter then
than I am now, and my falls were not likely to be serious :—" My father, on hearing a *thump*, would turn his
head half aside, and say,—' Take care of thy money,
lad.' "

MODERN LEARNING,

Exemplified in the form of a College Examination,

A JEU D'ESPRIT,

said to be written by the late PROFESSOR PORSON; and
intended as a *Satire* on the mode of Examination at
Oxford.

METAPHYSICS.

Professor..—What is a salt-box?
Student.—It is a box made to contain salt.
Professor.—How is it divided?
Student.—It is a salt-box, and a box of salt.
Professor.—Very well; show the distinction?

Student. A salt-box may be where there is no salt, but salt is absolutely necessary to the existence of a box of salt.

Professor.—Are not salt-boxes otherwise divided ?

Student.—Yes, by a partition.

Professor.—What is the use of this division?

Student.—To separate the *coarse* from the *fine.*

Professor.—How ! Think a little.

Student.—To separate the *fine* from the *coarse.*

Professor.—To be sure : to separate the *fine* from the coarse. But are not salt-boxes otherwise distinguished ?

Student.—Yes, into possible, probable, and positive.

Professor.—Define these several kinds of salt-boxes.

Student.—A possible salt-box is a salt-box yet unsold, in the joiner's hands.

Professor.—Why so ?

Student.—Because it hath not yet become a salt-box, having never had any salt in it, and it may probably be applied to some other use.

Professor.—Very true ; for a salt-box which never had, hath not now, and perhaps may never have, any salt in it, can only be termed a possible salt-box. What is a probable salt-box ?

Student.—It is a salt-box in the hands of one going to buy salt, and who has sixpence in his pocket to pay the shopkeeper ; and a positive salt-box is one which hath actually and *bonâ fide* got salt in it.

Professor.—Very good; and what other divisions of the salt-box do you recollect ?

Student.—They are divided into *substantive* and *pendent.* A substantive salt-box is that which stands by itself on a table or dresser ; and the pendent is that which hangs against the wall.

c

Professor.—What is the *idea* of a salt-box?

Student.—It is that image which the mind conceives of a salt-box, when no salt-box is present.

Professor.—What is the *abstract* idea of a salt-box?

Student.—It is the idea of a salt-box *abstracted* from the [idea of a box, or of salt, or of a salt-box, or of a box of salt.

Professor.—Very right : by this you may acquire a proper knowledge of a salt-box : but tell me, is the idea of a salt-box a *salt idea?*

Student.—Not unless the idea hath the idea of salt contained in it.

Professor.—True : and therefore an *abstract* idea cannot be either *salt or fresh, round or square, long or short :* and this shows the difference of a salt idea, and an idea of salt. Is an aptitude to hold salt an *essential* or an *accidental* property of a salt-box?

Student.—It is essential : but if there should be a crack in the bottom of the box, the aptitude to spill salt would be termed an accidental property of that box.

Professor.—Very well, very well indeed. What is the salt called with respect to the box?

Student.—It is called its contents.

Professor.—Why so?

Student.—Because the cook is content, *quod hoc,* to find plenty of salt in the box.

Professor.—You are very right. Now let us proceed to—

LOGIC.

Professor.—How many *modes* are there in a salt-box?

Student.—Three : bottom, top, and sides.

Professor.—How many modes are there in salt-boxes?

Student.—Four : the *formal*, the *substantive*, the *accidental*, and the *topsyturvy*.

Professor.—Define these several modes.

Student.—The formal respects the figure or shape of the box, such as a *circle*, a *square*, an *oblong*, &c. ; the substantive respects the work of the joiner; and the accidental respects the string by which the box is hung against the wall.

Professor.—Very well : what are the consequences of the accidental mode ?

Student.—If the *string* should break, the box would fall, and the salt be spilt, the salt-box broken, and the cook in a passion; and this is the accidental mode and its consequences.

Professor.—How do you distinguish between the bottom and top of a salt-box ?

Student.—The top of a salt-box is that part which is uppermost, and the bottom is that which is lowest in all positions.

Professor.—You should rather say, the uppermost part is the top, and the lowest part the bottom. How is it, then, if the *bottom* should be *uppermost ?*

Student.—The top would then be lowermost, so that the bottom would become the top, and the top the bottom ; and this is called the *topsyturvy* mode, and is nearly allied to the accidental, and frequently arises from it.

Professor.—Very good : but are not salt-boxes sometimes single, and sometimes double ?

Student.—Yes.

Professor.—Well, then, mention the several combinations of salt-boxes, with respect to the having *salt or not.*

Professor.—Hold ! Hold ! You are going too far.

Governors of the Institution.—We can't allow further time for logic ; proceed, if you please, to—

NATURAL PHILOSOPHY.

Professor.—What is a salt-box?

Student.—It is a combination of matter, fitted, framed, and joined, by the hands of a workman, in the form of a box, and adapted for the purpose of receiving and containing salt.

Professor.—Very good.   What are the *mechanical powers* engaged in the construction of a salt-box?

Student.—The *axe*, the *saw*, the *plane*, and the *hammer*.

Professor.—How are these powers applied to the purpose intended ?

Student.—The *axe* to fell the trees, the *saw* to split the timber, the—

Professor.—Consider ! It is the property of the mallet and wedge to split.

Student.—The *saw* to slit the timber, and the *plane* to smooth and thin the boards.

Professor.—How!   Take time, take time.

Student.—To thin and smooth the boards.

Professor.—To be sure : the boards are first thinned and then smoothed.   Go on.

Student.—The plane to thin and smooth, and the hammer to drive the nails.

Professor.—Or rather tacks.   Have not some *philosophers* considered *glue* as one of the mechanical powers?

Student.—Yes ; and it is still so considered : but it is called an inverse mechanical power ; because, whereas it is the property of direct mechanical powers to generate motion.   *Glue*, on the contrary, prevents motion, by keeping the parts to which it is applied fixed to each other.

Professor.—Very true. What is the mechanical law of the *saw?*

Student.—The power is to resist as the number of teeth and *force* impressed, multiplied by the number of strokes in a given time.

Professor.—Is the *saw* only used in slitting timber into boards?

Student.—Yes; it is also used in cutting boards into lengths.

Professor.—Not lengths. A thing cannot be said to be cut into lengths.

Student.—Shortnesses.

Professor.—Very right. What are the mechanical laws of the *hammer?*

Governor.—We have just received intelligence that dinner is nearly ready; and as the medical class is yet to be examined, let the medical gentlemen come forward.

THE COLLEGIAN AND THE PORTER.

At Trin. Coll. Cam.—which means, in proper spelling,
   Trinity College, Cambridge—there resided
One Harry Dashington; a youth excelling
   In all the learning commonly provided
      For those who choose that classic station
      For finishing their education.
That is—he understood computing.
   The odds at any race or match;
Was a dead hand at pigeon-shooting;
   Could kick up rows, knock down the watch.

Play truant and the rake at random,
Drink, tie cravats, and drive a tandem.

Remonstrance, fine, and rustication,
So far from working reformation,
  Seemed but to make his lapses greater ;
Till he was warned that next offence
Would have this certain consequence,——
  Expulsion from his *Alma Mater.*

One need not be a necromancer,
  To guess that, with so wild a wight,
  The next offence occurr'd next night ;
  When our incurable came rolling
  Home as the midnight chimes were tolling,
And rang the college bell.——No answer.

The second peal was vain—the third
  Made the street echo its alarum ;
When, to his great delight, he heard,
  The sordid *Janitor*, old Ben,
  Rousing and growling in his den.
' Who's there ?—I 'spose young Harum-scarum.'
  " 'Tis I, my worthy Ben—'tis Harry."
  " Aye, so I thought, and there you'll tarry.

' 'Tis past the hour—the gates are closed ;
  You know my orders—I shall lose
    My place if I undo the door."
' And I,"——(young hopeful interposed)
  Shall be *expelled* if you refuse ;
    So, pr'ythee"———Ben began to snore.

" I'm wet," cried Harry, " to the skin,
   Hip ! hallo ! Ben !—don't be a ninny ;
   Beneath the gate I've thrust a guinea,
So tumble out, and let me in."
" Humph !" growled the greedy old curmudgeon,
Half overjoyed, and half in dudgeon,
   " Now you may pass ; but make no fuss,
On tiptoe walk, and hold your prate."
   " Look on the stones, old Cerberus,"
Cried Harry, as he passed the gate ;
   " I've dropped a shilling—take the light,
You'll find it just outside—good night."

Behold the porter in his shirt,
   Cursing the rain, which never stopped,
Groping and raking in the dirt,
     And all without success ; but that
     Is hardly to be wondered at,
   Because no shilling had been dropped ;
So he gave o'er the search at last,
Regained the door, and found it fast !

With sundry oaths and growls and groans,
   He rang once—twice—and thrice ; and then,
Mingled with giggling, heard the tones
   Of Harry mimicking old Ben.

" Whose there ?—'Tis really a disgrace
   To ring so loud—I've locked the gate—
   I know my duty—'tis too late—
You wouldn't have me lose my place ?"
   " Pshaw ! Mr. Dashington ; remember
   This is the middle of November.

I'm stripped ;—'tis raining cats and dogs."
" Hush, hush !" quoth Hal ; " I'm fast asleep ;"
And then he snored as loud and deep
    As a whole company of hogs.
" But, hark ye, Ben, I'll grant admittance
    At the same rate I paid myself."
" Nay, master, leave me half the pittance,"
    Replied the avaricious elf.

" No ; all or none—a full acquittance ;—
    The terms, I know, are somewhat high ;
    But you have fixed the price, not I—
I won't take less—I can't afford it ;"
    So, finding all his haggling vain,
    Ben, with a oath and groan of pain,
Drew out the guinea, and restored it.

" Surely you'll give me," growled th' outwitted
Porter, when again admitted,
    " Something, now you've done your joking,
For all this trouble, time, and soaking."
    " Oh ! surely, surely," Harry said,
" Since, as you urge, I broke your rest,
And you're half drown'd and quite undress'd,
    I'll give you—leave to go to bed !"

N. M. M.

INTREPIDITY, ABILITY, AND ROGUERY.

On the sudden elevation of Bonaparte to the supreme
direction of affairs in the French republic, Dr. Paley observed to a party of gentlemen who were dining with
him a few days after the intelligence of that extraordinary

event, " That the French were rapidly approaching to absolute monarchy again : the conventional government was established on a very broad basis, which has been narrowed on every subsequent alteration, and is progressively tending to a point." In allusion to the various actors who had successively filled the busy scene, in that distracted country, from the commencement of the revolution, he still more forcibly remarked, " That in similar convulsions, none can ultimately succeed in bearing sway, but men of great *intrepidity*, great *ability*, and great *roguery*. Without great intrepidity, no man will intentionally venture on so hazardous a career; without great ability, no man can get forward ; and without great roguery, no man can bring his designs to a successful close."

THE ART OF APPLYING FIRE.

A certain Cantab, who was fellow of a college, and resided a short distance from the town in a neighbouring village, was suspected, by some of his *bons vivans*, of keeping a certain *fille de joie*, and with which they had often accused him ; but he invariably denied the fact. They, however, resolved to adopt some plan to unravel the mystery. At length, one of the party, in concert with another of their joint companions, who was *un bel esprit*, with all his wits about him, hit upon the following expedient for ascertaining the fact, viz. :—That he and his companions should, at midnight, proceed to the village on horse-back, where resided their friend, taking with them a *bundle of wet straw*. This they did, being especially provided with every necessary for carrying their design into effect. After having reconnoitred the outposts, lest they should be taken by surprise, finding all quiet, they placed the *wet straw* under the window of their unsuspecting friend, who was fast locked, either in the arms of Morpheus or *mademoiselle*. Having fired the straw, they set out shouting, with stentorian voices, " *Fire, fire, fire !*" This soon alarmed the enamoured pair, and the stratagem succeeded to their utmost wishes ; for, in a few moments, *mon cher ami* rushed from the house, with no covering on but his *shirt*, followed close by his *inamorata*, veiled in her *chemise*.

PRAYER FOR AN ENEMY.

A Cantab, having been offended by the mayor of Cambridge, who was by trade a butcher, resolved to take an opportunity of being even with him, when it came to his turn to preach before the corporation. This happening soon after, in his *prayer* before the *sermon*, he introduced the following pointed expressions :—" And since, O Lord ! thou hast commanded us to pray for our enemies, herein we beseech thee for the right worshipful the mayor : give him the strength of Samson and the courage of David ; that he may knock down sin like an ox, and cut the throat of iniquity like a suckling-calf ; and let his *horn* be exalted above his brethren."

CHARACTERISTICS.

Dr. Richard Farmer, the celebrated commentator on Shakspeare, was formerly master of Emanuel College,

Cambridge. He was very remarkable for many eccentricities, and made his likes and dislikes so well known, that they became almost a proverb in his days. There were three things, it was said, which the master of Emanuel loved above all others, viz. :—*Good old port ! old clothes !* and *old books !* And three things which nobody could persuade him to perform, viz. :—*To rise in the morning ! to go to bed at night !* and *to settle an account !* When in Cambridge, if an old house was pulled down, the master of Emanuel was always there, in an old blue great-coat and rusty hat. When in London, he was sure to be found in the same garb at an old book-stall ; or standing at the corner of a dirty lane, poring through his glass at an old play-bill. It is related, that Pitt once offered him a bishopric ; but the social delights of a pipe and a bottle in Emanuel parlour outweighed, in his estimation, the dazzling splendour of a *mitre.* He is said to have possessed that species of generosity which results rather from inattention than from a knowledge of the use of wealth ; but it seems he parted with his money as easily as he obtained it. To his honour be it spoken, many a person in distress experienced his liberality ; and it was frequently bestowed on learned men and learned publications, of which he was the unwearied patron.

A FORTUNATE EXPEDIENT.

A gentleman of Trinity College, travelling through France with a friend, in what, on that side of the water, was called a chaise, was very much teased with the mode of travelling, particularly as they made so little progress, and he wanted to reach the next town at a set time. He

tried gentle means of persuasion to induce the postillion
to urge his steeds, but in vain.   After floundering about
in French, till he was out of all patience, for he was no
great dab at it, and, withal, not being in possession of
any of those *emphatic* phrases which are equivalent to
such as Englishmen are accustomed to vent their anger
in, he bethought himself, that, if he was not understood,
he might at least frighten the fellow by using some high-
sounding words; and, collecting all the powers of elo-
quence of which he was master, with the voice of a
stentor, he roared into the ear of the postillion :—
" *Westmoreland, Cumberland, Northumberland, Durham!*" which the fellow mistaking for some tremendous
oath, accompanied with a threat, had the desired effect,
and induced him to increase his speed.

NOVEL INSCRIPTION.

A bishop of Exeter, having established a poor-house
for twenty-five old women, one day being in conversation
with Lord Mansfield, soon after, the bishop asked his
lordship for an inscription to place in front of the building, upon which his lordship directly took out his pencil, and wrote on a slip of paper as follows :—

" Under this roof
The Lord Bishop of Exeter
Keeps
Twenty-five Women."

QUOTING.

Porson, having spent an evening at a friend's house, a short distance from town, was brought the next morning to visit his friend's neighbour, who had a learned library, and a house full of books ; and, after apologizing for his dress and shoes, which were not his own, but supplied with the rest of his clothes by his companion (he having got wet through the night previous), and quoting Horace in two places for the awkwardness of a shoe too tight or too loose, and Theophrastus and Theocritus, he provoked one of the company to observe, " That the way to make the greatest expedition was to run, as the French and Dutch and Scotch women do, with their slippers in their hands, when they are pressed for time ;" and quoted Æschylus, where it is said in the Prometheus, " I hurried out of the carriage without sandals." Upon this, Porson started up upon his feet, and, fired, as a strict sportsman is when he hears a strange gun in the preserve which he keeps for his own shooting, no sooner were the three words pronounced, than he gave Stanley's comment and parallel passages upon them ; for such was the local mechanism of his memory, that, mention a line in any classic, and he would not only tell what followed, but the subsequent clause. But to proceed : he quoted a similar passage from Bion, which, consisting of a broken line, a whole verse, and a broken one, he made the most of them, and thundered them out with a menacing gesture, and a strong emphasis on the last words, " without sandals." The gentleman, who had innocently begun the match, and had never seen Porson before in a room, was struck with the earnestness of his manner and apparent displeasure, and determined neither to give up nor sit still, but to follow the professor, and do as he did; he therefore, too, stood upon his legs, and roared out, in the words of the next quotation in Stanley from Theocritus, " Arise, nor stay to put the sandals on your feet." The professor was startled to find his opponent on the same ground with himself, and so near at his heels; but, doubting if it were not by mere accident, he took the next passage from Horace that followed in the commentator, to which he added the remark of Stanley that concludes his note: namely, " that water-nymphs went unshod, and for that reason Homer gives Thetis the epithet of silver-footed," and here, for he was in the habit of seeing every body and every thing out, as usual, he had the last word.

THE PETITION.

Dr. Boldero, formerly master of Jesus College, had been treated with great severity by the protectorate for his attachment to the royal cause, as was Herring, at that time Bishop of Ely, and in whose gift the mastership of Jesus College is vested. On a vacancy of the mastership occurring, Boldero, without any pretensions to the appointment, in plain English plucks up his spirits, or, in Homer's language, *speaks to his magnanimous soul,** and presents his *petition* to the bishop. " Who are you?" says his lordship, " I know nothing of you! I never heard of you before!" " My lord," replied Boldero, " I have suffered long and severely for my at-

---

* ———————— ειπε προς μεγαλητορα θυμον.

tachment to my royal master, as well as your lordship, and I believe your lordship and I have been in all
the *gaols* in England." " What does the fellow mean !"
exclaimed the bishop, " Man! I never was confined in
any *prison* but the *Tower !"* " And, my Lord," said
Boldero, " I have been in all the rest myself!" The
bishop's heart was melted at this reply, and he granted
Boldero's petition.

THE PRESIDENT

Of a certain college in Cambridge was one evening
listening at the door of one of the under-graduates of his
college, suspecting something improper to be proceeding within. The student, by some means having acquired a knowledge of the snare, taking the *pot de cham-
bre* in his hand, he suddenly opened his door and discharged the contents over the president, accompanied
with a kick, exclaiming, at the same time, " Get down,
you rascal ! I'll tell the president of your listening at
my door !"

STOMACHUM.

When Morton, afterwards Bishop of Durham, stood
for the degree of D.D. at Cambridge, he advanced something which was displeasing to the professor, who exclaimed, with some warmth, " Commosti mihi stoma-
chum !" To which Morton replied, " Gratulor tibi, re-
verende professor, de bono tuo stomacho, canabis apud
me hâc nocte."

MAPS.

Mr. John Nicholson, formerly a well-known book-seller in Cambridge (a full length portrait of whom, painted by Reinagle, hangs in the entrance to the public library), originally hawked *prints* and *maps* round the colleges for sale, and it was his custom to bawl at the entrance to the staircases which led to the rooms where the students kept, " Maps!" From this circum-stance he was, by the gownsmen, so named; and the following hexameter was circulated through the Univer-sity on the occasion :—

Μαπς αυτον κηλιυσι θιοι, ανδρεσδε Νιχολσον.

TRANSLATED.

Snobs call him Nicholson! a plebeian name,
Which ne'er would hand a snobite down to fame,
But to posterity he'll go,—perhaps,
Since Granta's classic sons have dubbed him *Maps!*

PRIOR.

Prior kept his fellowship of St. John's College, Cam-bridge, till his death, and used to say—' The *salary* will always insure me a *bit of mutton and a clean shirt!*"

SILLY-BUBB.

Lord Melcombe, when his name was plain *Bubb*, was intended by the administration of that time to be sent ambassador to Spain. While this matter was in contemplation, Lord Chesterfield met him, and, touching him upon the proposed embassy, told Bubb, that he did not, by any means, think him fit to be the representative of the crown of England, at the Spanish court. Bubb begged to know the ground of his objection : ' Why," said his lordship, " your name is too short. Bubb, Bubb,—do you think the Spaniards, a people who pride themselves on their family honours, and the length of their titles, will suppose a man can possess any dignity or importance, with a name of one syllable, which can be pronounced in a second? No, my friend, you must not think of Spain, unless you make some addition to your name!" Bubb desired his lordship to say what he would have him do. Lord Chesterfield, pausing a moment, exclaimed,—" I have it : what do you think of calling yourself *Silly-Bubb?*"

DROPSICAL.

From the number of *bores* made in Cambridge, your attention is not unfrequently attracted by a small fountain playing. Some gentlemen one day discoursing on the subject, it was facetiously observed by Dr. G——, then Vice-Chancellor, " that, although Cambridge had been *tapped* very often, it was still very dropsical!"

WISEACRES.

Ben Jonson, being one evening at a tavern-club, seated at the upper end of the table, amongst his inge-

D

nious sons, and talking of nothing but poetry, was often interrupted by a country gentleman, who would permit no other discourse to pass about than what tended to tillage and husbandry; what rich pasture ground was in his county, the price of corn, and the care of cattle. This so incensed old Ben, that he could forbear no longer, but let fly at him in his language. "Thou clod," said Ben, "why dost thou mingle thy dirty discourse with our sublime fancies? I tell thee, for every acre thou hast of land, I have ten acres of wit!" "Have you so, Sir," replied the gentleman; "I cry your mercy, good *Mister Wise-Acres!*" Ben Jonson was so highly taken with the jest, that he swore he was never so pricked by a *hobnail* in all his life.

VERY EASY TO WRITE LIKE A FOOL.

Lee, the dramatist, who was educated at Trinity College, was confined four years of his short life in Bedlam. When a sane idiot of a scribbler mocked his calamity, and observed that it was easy to write like a madman; Lee answered, "No, sir, it is not easy to write like a madman, but very easy to write like a fool!"

THE BRASS PLATE.

The first year that "*Poor Robin's Almanack*" came forth (about A D. 1666), there was cut for it a brass plate, having on one side of it the pictures of King Charles the First, the Earl of Stafford, the Archbishop of Canterbury, the Earl of Derby, the Lord Capel, and

Doctor Hewit; all six adorned with wreaths of laurel
On the other side was Oliver Cromwell, Bradshaw
Ireton, Scott, Harrison, and Hugh Peters, hanging in
chains; betwixt which were placed the Earl of Esse:
and Mr. Christopher Love. Upon this plate, Mr
Lewis Griffin, a Cantab, wrote the following lines :—

Bless us! what have we here, what sundry shapes
Salute our eyes! Have martyrs too their *apes?*
Sure 'tis the war of angels, for you'd swear
That here stood *Michael*, and the *Dragon* there.
Tredescant is outvied, for we engage
Both Heaven and hell in an *octavo page*—
Martyrs and *traitors* rallied six to six,
Half fled unto *Olympus*, half to *Styx ;*
Joined with two *Neuters*, some condemn, some praise
They hang betwixt the *halters* and the *bays :*
For 'twixt *Noll's* torment and great Charles's glory
There, there's the *Presbyterian purgatory.*

SCRAPING THE PROCTOR.

A custom formerly prevailed of *scraping the procto*
or any other university officer, who had rendered him
self obnoxious by any particular measure. " I myself,
says Dr. Disney, in his memoirs of Dr. Jebb, " was on
of the offending gallery; but whether an offender c
not, I will not say, for I do not recollect, though to
prone to mischiefs of that kind." After a few names ha
been taken down, comes Mr. *Homer*, of Emanuel, no
deceased. " What is your name, Sir?" said Purkes:
the other proctor: " *Homer*, of Emanuel," was the reply

D 2

" Sir," .said the proctor, "you are attempting to impose upon me ! *Homer*, do you say ?" " Yes, Sir," he answered, " *Homer*, of Emanuel !" " Very well, Sir." After two or three more names, comes a gentleman of my year. " Your name, Sir ?" said the proctor. " *Pindar*, of Queen's !" was the answer. " Sir," vociferated the proctor, " I will not be insulted in this manner ? I insist upon it, Sir, that you tell me your name?" " My name is *Pindar*, of Queen's," was the reply, " and, if you don't like that, I have no other to give you !"

A TRANSPORTING SUBJECT.

The subject for the Chancellor's English Prize Poem, for the year 1823, was *Australasia* (New Holland.). This happened to be the subject of conversation at a party of Johnians, when some observing that they thought it a bad subject, one of the party remarked, " It was at least a *transporting* one."

COMPLETING A STANZA.

It is related that Dr. Mansel, then an undergraduate of Trinity College, Cambridge, by chance called at the rooms of a brother Cantab, who was absent ; but he had left on his table the opening of a poem, which was in the following lofty strain :—

> " The sun's perpendicular rays
> Illumine the depths of the sea ;"

Here the flight of the poet by some accident stopped

short ; but Dr. Mansel, who was seldom (if we may credit fame), lost on such occasions, illuminated the subject by completing the stanza in the following very facetious style :—

" The fishes, beginning to sweat,
    Cried d—n it, how hot we shall be !"

LORD CHESTERFIELD,

Who was educated at Trinity Hall, Cambridge, advised a nobleman who had just finished a magnificent mansion, extremely *inconvenient within*, but most *splendid without*, to rent the opposite house that he might enjoy the prospect.

HANGING ONE'S SELF.

Paley was always very fond of attending courts of law, to hear the trials. When a boy, he is said to have attended York assizes, to hear the trial of Eugene Aram, a man of extraordinary learning and acuteness. The trial was for the murder of Daniel Clark, and he was convicted on the evidence of Richard Houseman, an accomplice, and his own wife. The evidence brought forward, and the ingenious defence of Aram, made a strong impression on the mind of Paley. He seemed to attribute the conviction of the prisoner, in a very great measure, to his own defence ; for, many years after, when he was conversing with some friends about the lives of some obscure and undeserving persons having been inserted in the *Biographia Britannica*, and on one of the party exclaiming,—" Eugene Aram, for instance !"—" Nay," replied Paley, " a man that has been hanged has some pretensions to notoriety, and especially a man who has got himself hanged, as Eugene Aram did, by his own cleverness."

CURIOUS EPISTLE.

When Cromwell commissioned Lockhart against Dunkirk, he presented him with the following epistle, to be previously sent to Mazarine, commander of that fortress :

" Thou traitor, Mazarine, if thou dost refuse to deliver up Dunkirk unto Lockhart, my friend and counsellor, by the eternal God, I'll come and tear thee from thy master's bosom, and hang thee at the gates of Paris.
(Signed)   CROMWELL."

ALCOCK.

The device of John Alcock, founder of Jesus College and Bishop of Ely, is conspicuous in every part of that college, and is a *pun* upon his name. It is a *cock* perching upon a *globe*. On one window was a cock with a label from its mouth, with this inscription : Εγω ειμι αλεκτωρ. To which another, on the opposite side, bravely crows in answer—οντως και εγω :—

" ' I am a cock !" the one does cry :
And t'other answers—' So am I !' "

EPIGRAM.

At an examination in the University of Cambridge, the examiner, whose name was *Hawkes*, proved a very talkative man ; indeed, so much so, that some of the students, undergoing examination, requested one of their companions, rather famous for trite sayings, to make an epigram upon him. He immediately answered :—

> " Hawkes
> Talks!"

PORSON AND THE GERMANS.

Porson was a great master of *Iambic* measure, as he has shown us in the preface to the second edition of his Hecuba. The German critic, Herman, whom he makes to say, in his notes on the Medea,—" We Germans understand quantity better than the English," accuses the professor of being more dictatorial than explanatory, in his metrical decisions. Upon which the professor fired the following epigram against the German:—

Νηΐδες ἰστὶ μέτρων ὦ τευτονες, οὐχ ὁ μεν, ὡς δ'ου, Παντες πλην Ἐρμαννος, ὁ δ' Ἑρμαννος σφόρρα Τευτων.

> The Germans, in Greek,
> Are sadly to seek ;
> Not five in five score,
> But ninety-five more,—
> All, save only Herman,
> And Herman's a German.

DEFINITION OF HAPPINESS.

At an examination for the degree of B. A. in the Senate House, Cambridge, under an examiner whose name was *Payne*, one of the moral questions was— " Give a definition of happiness ?" To which one of the candidates returned the following laconic answer,— " An *exemption* from *Payne*." Some persons are so unfortunate as to buy their wit at a great price, as was proved in the above case ; for, on the gentleman declining to apologize to Mr. Payne, he was suspended from his *degree*, for a very considerable time.

ONE TONGUE SUFFICIENT FOR A WOMAN.

Milton was asked by a friend, " whether he would instruct his daughters in the *different languages?*" To which Milton replied,—" No, Sir, one tongue is sufficient for a woman !"

A NEW READING.

Towards the close of the administration of Sir Robert Walpole, he was talking very freely to some of his friends of the vanity and vexations of office; and, alluding to his intended retirement, quoted from Horace the following passage :—

" Lusisti satis, edisti satis, atque bibisti :
Tempus abire tibi est."

" Pray, Sir Robert," said one of his friends, " is that

good Latin?" "Why, I think so," answered Sir Robert "what objection have you to it?" "Why," said the othe drily, "I did not know but the word might be *bribe-is* in your Horace."

A SAYING OF LORD BACON.

James the First, King of England, asked Lord Chan cellor Bacon,—"What he thought of the French am bassador?" His lordship replied,—"that he was a tal proper man." "Aye," said his majesty, "but wha think you of his headpiece?"—"Sir," said Lord Bacon tall men are like high houses, wherein commonly the up permost rooms are worst furnished."

CATHERINE HALL.

A lady, whose nephew was a student at Cambridge meeting a Cantab, an acquaintance, asked him, hov he conducted himself?" "Why truly, madam," wa the reply, "he is a brave fellow, and sticks close t Catherine Hall?" "I protest," said she, "I feared a much; he was always hankering after the *wenches* fron a boy!"

NEWTON.

Sir Isaac is reported to have said, a little before h expired—"I don't know what I may seem to the world but, as to myself, I seem to have been only like a bo playing on the sea-shore, and diverting myself by nov and then finding a smoother pebble, or a prettier shel than ordinary, whilst the *great ocean* of *truth* lay all un discovered before me."

STERNE

Was bred at Jesus College, Cambridge, where it is
said he studied very little, laughed a great deal, and was
particularly fond of puzzling his tutors.   He left Cambridge with the character of being singular, without guile,
and possessed of considerable talents whenever he thought
proper to use them.   The following is a tale told by himself:—"I happened," said he, "to be acquainted with a
young man who had been bound apprentice to a stationer
in Yorkshire; he had just then finished his time, set up
in London, and rented a window in one of the flagged
alleys in the city.   I hired one of the panes of glass from
my friend, and stuck upon it, with a wafer, the following

"'ADVERTISEMENT.

"'Epigrams, Anagrams, Paragrams, Chronograms,
Monograms, Epitaphs, Epithilamiums, Prologues, Epi-
logues, Madrigals, Interludes, Advertisements, Letters,
Petitions, Memorials on every occasion, Essays on all
subjects, Pamphlets for or against Ministry, with Sermons
upon any Text, or for any Sect, to be written here on
reasonable terms, by   A. B. PHILOLOGER.

"The uncommonness of the titles occasioned numerous applications; and at length I used privately to glide
into my office to digest the notes or heads of the day, and
to receive the earnings, which were always directed to be
left with the memorandums; the writing to be paid for
on delivery, according to the subject.   The ocean of
vice and folly," says Sterne, "that opened itself to my
view during the time continued this odd department of

my life, shocked and disgusted me so much, that the very moment I realized a small sum, and discharged the rent of my pane, I closed the horrid scene."

THE FOX.

A student of St. John's College, who was remarkable for his larks and eccentricities, during the time he was dining in hall, called to a *bon-vivant* at another table, to say, " that he had got a fine *fox* in his rooms, for him!" This being overheard by the *marker*, who was a kind of mongrel fetch-and-carry to a certain dean, and who understood the student in a literal sense, he took an early opportunity to inform the dean of the circumstance. The student was very soon summoned before the master and seniors, for what he knew not ; however, on entering, he was informed, " they had learned he kept a *fox* in his rooms—a thing not to be tolerated by the college." " It is very true," replied the accused ; " I have a *bust* of CHARLES JAMES FOX, at your service ! "

DEFINITION OF A FELLOWSHIP

Through an avenue of trees, at the back of Trinity College, a church may be seen at a considerable distance, the approach to which affords no very pleasing scenery. The late Professor Porson, on a time, walking that way with a friend, and observing the church, remarked, " That it put him in mind of a *fellowship*, which was a long dreary walk, with a church at the end of it."

"I CAN GET THROUGH."

In the cloisters of Trinity College, beneath the library, are grated windows, through which many of the students have occasionally, after the gates were locked, taken the liberty of passing, without an *exeat*, in rather a novel style. It so happened that, as a certain Cantab was in the act of drawing himself through the bars, he being more than an ordinary mortal's bulk, he stuck fast; and, whilst he was in this dilemma, one of the fellows of the college was passing by, who, stepping up to the student, asked him, in rather an ironical tone, " if he should assist him ?" " Thank you," was the reply, " I can get through !" At the same instant he drew himself on the outside.

FAWKES.

Francis, an ingenious poet and divine, was educated at Jesus College, where he took his degrees in arts. He obtained the united vicarages of Orpington and St. Mary Cray, in Kent. He has jocosely related the stratagem he employed to acquire these livings. Dr. Herring was then Archbishop of Canterbury, and Mr. Fawkes, having written a few miscellaneous subjects, committed them to the press, and published them. He made choice of the archbishop for his patron, and prefixed to his poetical labours a dedication to that prelate. Pleased with the compositions of the young poetical divine, his grace honoured him with a general invitation to his table, and added, " the oftener I see you, I shall be more obliged to you." " I took him at his word," says Fawkes, " and

engaged lodgings at Lambeth, and dined with his lordship every day, for upwards of three-quarters of a year.
During that time, however, many hints were given me,
that my visits were too frequent; but I never thought
proper to understand them, the archbishop's general and
unqualified promise being a sufficient warrant for my
presence. In a word, I stuck so close to him, and per-
secuted him so much with my company, that he gave me
the livings merely to get rid of me."

BEN JONSON,

When the archbishop of York sent him from his table
an excellent dish of fish, but without drink, said—

"In a dish came fish
From the arch-bis-
Hop was not there,
Because there was no *beer*."

SMART'S SAYING OF GRAY.

Those who remember Mr. Gray when at the University of Cambridge, where he resided the greater part o
his life, will recollect that he was a little prim fastidiou
man, distinguished by a short shuffling step. He commonly held up his gown behind with one of his hands
at the same time cocking up his chin, and perking up hi
nose. Christopher Smart, who was contemporary wit
him at Pembroke Hall, used to say that "Gray walke
as if he had fouled his small-clothes, and looked as if h
smelt it."

BALLAD-SINGING.

Dr. Richard Corbet, Bishop of Norwich, was a great humourist in his words and actions. "After he was D. D." says Aubrey, "he sang ballads at the Crosse at Abingdon. On a market-day, he and some of his companions were at the taverne by the Crosse (which by the way was one of the finest in England). A ballad-singer complained that he had no custome; he could not put off his ballads. The jolly doctor puts off his gowne and puts on the ballad-singer's leathern jacket, and, being a handsome man, and having a rare full voice, he presently vended a great manye, and had a great audience."

RIDING HIS OWN HORSE.

There was a society established at Cambridge, in the year 1757, by the Wranglers, when Dr. Waring was senior, and Mr. Jebb second, called " *The Hyson Club.*" The members were accustomed to meet for the purpose of drinking tea, and holding rational conversation. Several of the highest characters in the university were already enrolled amongst its members, when Doctor, then Mr. Paley, became an associate, soon after his establishment in the tuition of Christ College. No particular subjects of discussion were proposed at their meetings, but accident, or the taste of the individuals, naturally led to topics, in which literary men might fairly unbend themselves from severer pursuits. In a debate, one evening, on the justice and expediency of making some alteration in the ecclesiastical constitution of this country, for the relief of tender consciences, Doctor Gordon, fellow of Emanuel College, and afterwards precentor of Lincoln, an avowed Tory in religious politics, when vehemently opposing the arguments of Mr. Jebb, a strenuous supporter of all such improvements, exclaimed, with his usual heat;—"You mean, Sir, to impose upon us a new church government." "You are mistaken, Sir," said Mr. Paley,—"Jebb only wants to ride his own horse, not to force you to get up behind him."

WAY OF USING BOOKS.

Sterne used to say—"The most accomplished way of using books is to serve them as some people do lords, learn their titles and then brag of their acquaintance."

TROPHIES.

A French nobleman once showing Matthew Prior the palace of his master at Versailles, and desiring him to observe the many *trophies* of Louis the Fourteenth's victories, asked Prior, if King William, his master, had many such trophies in his palace. "No," said Prior, "the monuments of my master's victories are to be seen everywhere but in his own house."

THE COST OF FASHION.

Lord Mansfield, being willing to save a man who had stolen a watch, desired the jury to value it at *ten-pence;*

upon which the prosecutor cried out, "*ten-pence*, my lord,—why the very *fashion* of it cost me *five pounds!*" "Oh," says his lordship, "we must not hang a man for *fashion's sake!*"

POPISH ZEAL.

The Popish party, not content with the indignities they had heaped upon the person of Archbishop Cranmer, actually burnt, publicly, his book on the sacrament. This being told him, he exclaimed, "Ah! they have honoured it more than it deserved, for I hear they burnt it with the *New Testament*." Which was the fact.

COMPLAINT AND WISH.

Dryden's wife complained to him that he was always reading, and took little notice of her, and finished her complaint with saying, " I wish I was a book, and then I should enjoy more of your company." "Yes, my dear," said Dryden, " I wish you were a book—but an *Almanack*, I mean, for then I should change you every year.

QUAINT EPITAPH.

Doctor Fuller having requested one of his companions, who was a *bon-vivant*, to make an epitaph for him, received the following, with the conceit of which he always expressed himself much pleased,—

"*Here lies Fuller's earth!*"

PATIENCE.

A fellow of Trinity College, Cambridge, on the eve of his departure from the university, preached at St. Mary's upon these words—"*Have patience with me, and I will pay you all*;" and, owing a large sum of money in the town, enlarged mightily on the first part of the text,— "Have patience." "Now," says he, "I should come to the second part of the text, *and I will pay you all;* but, having pressed too long on your *patience*, I must leave that till the next opportunity ; so pray have patience with me !"

BUT ONE GOOD TRANSLATION.

Dryden's translation of Virgil being commended by a right reverend bishop, Lord Chesterfield said, " The original is indeed excellent; but everything suffers by a translation—except a bishop !"

"THERE I LEAVE YOU."

The witty and licentious Earl of Rochester, meeting with the great and learned Isaac Barrow in the Park, told his companion that he would have some fun with the rusty old pot. Accordingly, he went up with great gravity, and, taking off his hat, made the doctor a profound bow, saying, " Doctor, I'm your's to my shoe-tie." The doctor, seeing his drift, immediately pulled off his beaver, and returned the bow, with, " My lord, I'm your's to the

E

ground." Rochester followed up his salutation by a deeper bow, saying, "Doctor, I am your's to the centre." Barrow, with a very lowly obeisance, replied, "My lord, I am your's to the Antipodes." His lordship, nearly gravelled, exclaimed, "Doctor, I am your's to the lowest pit of hell!" "*There*, my lord," said Barrow, sarcastically, "*I'll leave you!*" and walked off.

JUDGMENT.

James the Second, when Duke of York, made a visit to Milton the poet, and asked him, amongst other things, if he did not think the loss of his sight a *judgment* upon him for what he had written against his father, Charles the First. Milton answered,—"If your Highness think my loss of sight a *judgment* upon me, what do you think of your father's losing his head?"

QUEERING A FULL-BOTTOM.

Lord Mansfield used to relate the following anecdote of himself, with great good-humour. A St. Giles's bird appeared before him as an evidence in some trial concerning a quarrel in the street, and so confounded his lordship with *slang*, that he was obliged to dismiss him without getting anything from him. Being desired to give an account of all he knew, "My lord," says he, "as I was coming by the corner of a street, I *stagged* the man." "Pray," said Lord Mansfield, "what is *stagging* a man?" "Stagging, my lord,—why you see I was *down upon him*." "Well, but I don't understand *down upon him*, any more than *stagging* ; do speak to be understood." "Why, an't please your lordship, I speak as well as I can ; I was *up*, you see, to *all he knew*." "To all he knew,—I'm as much in the dark as ever." "Well then, my lord, I'll tell you how it was." "Do so." "Why, my lord, seeing as how he was a *rum kid*, I was *me upon his tibby*." The fellow, being at length sent out of court, his lordship not being able to make anything of his jargon, was heard in the hall to say to one of his companions—"that he had *gloriously queered* old *full-bottom !*"

THE TOBACCO-STOPPER.

It is said that Sir Isaac Newton did once in his life go a wooing, and, as was to be expected, had the greatest indulgence paid to his little peculiarities, which ever accompany a great genius. Knowing that he was fond of smoking, the lady assiduously provided him with a pipe, and they were seated as if to open the business of Cupid. Sir Isaac smoked a few whiffs—seemed at a loss for something—whiffed again—and at last drew his chair near to the lady : a pause of some minutes ensued ; he seemed a little uneasy ; "Oh the timidity of some !" thought the lady—when, lo ! Sir Isaac had got hold of her hand. The lady cast her eyes down towards the floor, and the palpitations began : he will *kiss* it, thought she, no doubt, and then the matter will be settled. Sir Isaac whiffed with redoubled fury, and drew the captive hand near his *head ;* already the expected salute vibrated from the hand to the heart—when, pity the damsel, gentle reader ! Sir Isaac only raised the fair hand, to make the fore-finger what he much wanted—*a tobacco-stopper !*

THE FORCE OF SATIRE.

Jacob Johnson, the most eminent of his profession as a publisher, having refused to advance Dryden a sum of money for a work upon which he engaged, the incensed bard sent a message to him, and the following lines, adding, " Tell the dog that he who wrote these can write more:"

" With leering looks, bull-faced, and freckled face,
  With two left legs, and Judas-coloured hair,
  And frowzy pores, that taint the ambient air !"

Johnson felt the force of the description; and, to avoid a completion of the portrait, immediately sent the money.

EXTEMPORE LINES BY LORD CHESTERFIELD.

Lord Chesterfield, on viewing Lady M——, a reputed Jacobite, adorned with orange ribands at the anniversary ball at Dublin, in the memory of King William, thus addressed her,—

EXTEMPORE :—

" Thou little Tory, where's th e jest
  To wear those ribands in thy breast ;
  When that breast, betraying, shows
  The whiteness of the rebel rose ?"

TILLOTSON,

Who was then Archbishop of Canterbury, on King William's complaining of the shortness of his sermon, answered, " Sire, could I have bestowed more time upon t, it would not have been so long !"

THE POST-BOY

Dr. Roger Long, the famous astronomer, walking one lark evening with Mr. Bonfoy in Cambridge, and the atter coming to a short *post* fixed in the pavement, which n the earnestness of conversation he took to be a boy tanding in his way, said hastily, " Get out of my way, boy !" " That boy, Sir," said the doctor very drily, ' is a *post-boy*, who never turns out of his way for anybody."

PUNNING

Was, at least, no *crime* in the days of the first Stuarts : neither kings nor nobles were above it. The great Lord Bacon was reduced to such extreme poverty towards the latter end of his life, that he wrote to James the First, for assistance, in these words :—" Help me, dear sovereign lord and master, and pity me so far, that I, who have been born to a *bag*, be not now in my age forced in effect to bear a *wallet ;* nor that I, who desire to *live* to study, may be driven to study to *live*." The following, in a letter to Prince Charles, may not be so pardonable, particularly from so great a man :— wherein he hopes, " that, as the father was his *creator*, the son will be his *redeemer*."

THE POKER AND TONGS.

Porson's company, as may well be supposed, was courted by all ranks, from the combination-room to the cider-cellar, for he mixed with all, and was to be found in both; and it was who should assist at his evening lectures, and who should carry away most from the oracle. But sometimes it would happen, as it does to most men, that he was *bedevilled,* and, pulling a book out of his pocket, read only to himself; at other times he was violent, and, catching the *poker* out of the fire, brandished it over his head, to the terror of the company. Of this trick, however, he was cured, once for all, by a spark of fighting notoriety, who, on seeing Porson seize the *poker,* and not being used to a furious Greek, but in the play, snatched up the *tongs,* observing, two could play at that game. Upon this, the professor, with a sneer of his own, said, " I believe, if I should crack your skull, I should find it very empty." And if I should break your head," replied the Irishman, " I should find it full of maggots." This retort pleased Porson so much, that he returned the poker to the fire, and repeated a whole chapter of Roderick Random, analogous to the affair.

" EVER SINCE HE WAS A PUPPY."

There was a coffee-room at the principal inn where Sterne resided about the time he wrote his " Tristram Shandy," where gentlemen who frequented the house might read the newspapers: one of the greatest enjoy-nents of Sterne's life was spending an inoffensive hour in a snug corner of his room. There was a troop of horse at that time quartered in the town; one of the officers was a gay young man, spoiled by the free intercourse of the world, but not destitute of good qualities. This young gentleman was remarkable for his freedom of speech, and pointed reflections on the clergy. The modest Yorick was often obliged to hear toasts he could not approve, and conversations shocking to the ear of delicacy, and was frequently under the necessity of removing his seat or pretending deafness. The captain, resolving this conduct should no longer avail him, seated himself by Yorick, so as to prevent his retreat, and immediately began a profane indecent tale at the expense of the clerical profession, with his eyes steadfastly fixed on Yorick, who pretended not to notice his ill manners; when that became impossible, he turned to the military intruder, and gravely said, " Sir, I'll tell you my story. My father is an officer, and is so brave himself, that he is fond of everything else that is brave, even his dog. You must know we have at this time one of the finest creatures of his kind in the world, the most spirited, yet the best-natured that can be imagined; so lively that he charms everybody; but he has a cursed trick that throws a shade over all his good qualities." " Pray, what may that be?" interrogated the officer: " He never sees a clergyman, but he instantly flies at him," answered Yorick. " How long has he had that trick?" " Why, Sir," replied the divine, " ever since he was a puppy!" The man of war for once blushed, and, after a pause, said, " Doctor, I thank you for your hint: give me, your hand.; I will never rail at a parson again."

HEBREW.

A Cantab, when on a tour in the country, chanced to enter a strange church, and, after he had been seated some little time, another person was ushered into the same pew with him. The service had proceeded till the *psalms* were about to be read, when the stranger pulled out of his pocket a prayer-book, and offered to share it with the Cantab, though he perceived he had one in his hand. This generosity, the Cantab perceived, proceeded from a mere ostentatious display of his learning, as it proved to be in *Latin;* and he immediately declined the offer by saying, " Sir, I read nothing but *Hebrew!"*

THE WHITE LION.

The Rev. George Harvest accompanied his patron into France, and, during the necessary delay at some post-town, rambled after a bookseller's shop, and found one. There he amused himself awhile with his favourite companions, but at last reflected that his friends were in haste to depart, and might be much incommoded by his stay. He had forgot the name of the inn, and to expect *him* to find the road merely because he had travelled it before was to expect that *Theseus* should unravel the *Dædalean* labyrinth with the thread of *Ariadne.* Not a word of *French* could Harvest speak to be understood; but he recollected the sign of the inn was a *lion;* still how to make the bookseller comprehend this was the difficulty. Harvest, however, tall and sturdy, raised him-

self, to the no small terror of the bookseller, with pro-
jected and curvetting arms, into the formidable attitude
of a *lion-rampant;* and succeeded at length, by this happy effort, in suggesting to the imagination of the staring
Frenchman the idea of a *lion!* But another difficulty of
a more arduous nature now presented itself : there were
black, red, and *white lions;* of which last colour was
the *lion* in question. Now, no two-footed creature under
the sun could less exemplify the following maxim,—

" *That cleanliness is next to godliness,*"

than the hero of this adventure; for Harvest was
habitually very slovenly in his person. However, to
complete the aggregate, and impress the idea, not of a
lion only, but of a *white-lion,* upon the *sensorium* of
Monsieur, Harvest unbuttoned his waistcoat and display-
ed his *shirt* : but, alas ! like the *mulberry-tree* of old,—

" *Qui color albus erat nunc est contrarius albo.*"

This would have thrown but little light upon the subject,
had not the polite Frenchman put a right construction
upon the case, and extricated poor Harvest from his
difficulty by a safe conveyance to

THE WHITE-LION !

BILL PAID IN FULL.

At Wimpole, formerly the seat of Lord Oxford, but
now of Lord Hardwicke, there was to be seen a portrait

of Mr. Harley, the speaker, in his robes of office. The
active part he took to forward the bill to settle the
crown on the house of Hanover induced him to have a
scroll painted in his hand bearing the title of that bill.
Yet, soon after George the First arrived in England,
Harley was sent to the *Tower*. This circumstance being
told to Prior, whilst he was viewing the portrait, he took
a pencil out of his pocket, and wrote on the white part
of the scroll the date of the day on which Harley was
committed to the Tower, and under it,—

"THIS BILL PAID IN FULL."

GRAY,

The poet, wrote the following character of himself,
which was found in a pocket-book after his death :—

"Too poor for a bribe, and too proud to importune,
He had not the method of making a fortune :
Could love and could hate, so was thought somewhat odd,
No very great wit,—he believed in a God;
A post or a pension he did not desire,
But left church and state to Charles Townshend and Squire.

EPIGRAM.

Porson one day visiting his brother-in-law, Mr. P——,
who at that time lived in Lancaster Court, in the Strand,
found him indisposed, and under the influence of medicine. On returning to the house of a common friend,

ıe of course expected to be asked after the health of
ıis relation. After waiting with philosophic patience,
without the expected question being proposed, he reproached the company for not giving him an opportunity
of giving the following answer, which he had composed
ın his walk :—

" My Lord of Lancaster, when late I came from it,
   Was taking a medicine of names not a few ;
In Greek an emetic, in Latin a vomit,
   In English a puke, and in Vulgar a sp—w."

LATIMER,

The pious and learned martyr, and Bishop of Wor-
cester, who was educated at Christ College, Cambridge,
and was one of the first reformers of the church of
England, at a controversial conference, being out-talked
by younger divines, and out-argued by those who were
more studied in the *fathers*, said, " I cannot talk for my
religion, but I am ready to die for it."

WHITE TEETH.

Professor Saunderson, who occupied so distinguished
a situation in the University of Cambridge, as that of
Lucasian Professor of Mathematics, was *quite blind.*
Happening on a time to make one in a large party, he
remarked of a lady who had just left the room, but
whom he had never before met, nor heard of, that she
had very *white teeth.* The company were anxious to

learn how he had discovered this, which was very true. "I have reason," observed the professor, "to believe that the lady is not a *fool*, and I can think of no other motive for her laughing incessantly, as she did for a whole hour together."

JOHNIAN HOG.

The following, amongst other reasons, is given as the origin of the students of St. John's College being denominated *hogs*. A waggish genius espying a coffee-house waiter carrying a dish to a Johnian, who was seated in another box in the same coffee-house, asked, ' if it were a dish of grains?" The Johnian immediately replied,——

"Says ——, the Johns eat grains ; suppose it true,
They pay for what they eat ; does he so too ?"

"TUES PORCUS."

There is a custom in the University of Cambridge of *huddling*, as it is called, or keeping an act, after the degree of *A. B.* is conferred. It so happened, that a gentleman had to keep one, whose name was *Hogg*, under a moderator who was of St. John's College, the men of which college had obtained the appellation of *Johnian hogs,* as have the men of Trinity the appellation of *bull-dogs;* and many other names are applied to the men of the different colleges, for the origin of which here is little but traditional evidence. On Mr. Hogg's mounting the rostrum, he was addressed by the mode rator, " *Tu es porcus*," (thou art a hogg). To which Mr. Hogg retorted, " *Sed none grege porcorum*," (bu not of the herd of hogs).

NOVEL CONSTRUCTION OF A PAIR OF BELLOWS.

At an examination in the Senate House, Cambridge one of the questions given was, " to construct a pair o common bellows;" to which one of the students gav the following laconic answer:—" A pipe, two boards a piece of leather, and a hole to put your knee in."

BACON,

Sir Nicholas, who was educated at *Corpus Christi*, o Benet College, Cambridge, being visited at his house by Queen Elizabeth, she observed, alluding to his corpu lency, " that he had built his house too little for him." " Not so, Madam," answered he ; " but your Majesty has made me too big for my house."

PALEY'S CONCEPTION OF THE CHARACTER OF FALSTAFF.

Paley, when young, was particularly fond of theatrica exhibitions, especially when any eminent performer ap peared from the metropolis on the provincial board near where he resided. This predilection never for

ook him. In a provincial theatre, he always seated
himself as near as possible to the front of the centre box.
Conversing about the character of *Falstaff*, as delineated
by Shakespeare, he remarked, "That amongst actors it
was frequently misunderstood : he was a courtier of the
age he lived in ; a man of vivacity, humour, and wit ; a
great reprobate, but no buffoon."

VALUE OF NOTHING.

Porson was no less distinguished for his wit and
humour, during his residence in Cambridge, than for
his profound learning; and he would frequently divert
himself by sending quizzical *morceaux*, in the shape of
notes, to his companions. He one day sent his gyp
with a note to a certain Cantab, who is now a D. D. and
Master of his College, requesting him to find the value
of nothing ? Next day he met his friend walking, and,
stopping him, he desired to know, " Whether he had
succeeded?" His friend answered—" Yes !" " And
what may it be?" asked Porson : " *sixpence !*" replied the
Cantab, " which I gave the man for bringing the note."

SERMON.

Dr. Dodd's sermon, which was preached to some
Cambridge scholars extempore, from a hollow tree :—

(Copied from an old Tract.)

The following sermon was made and preached *extempore* by one *Parson Dodd,* who lived within three or

four miles of Cambridge, and who having for nigh half
a year, every Sunday, preached on the same subject
which was drunkenness, which gave some of the Cambridge scholars occasion to be displeased with him, who
thought he reflected upon them, they resolved to be
even with the doctor when an opportunity should offer.
Accordingly, chance one day led the doctor in their
way: a company of *scholars* being walking, they saw
the doctor some way off, coming towards them, and,
all stopping at a gate that hung to a hollow tree, the
doctor presently came up, and they spoke very friendly
to him. " Your servant, Mr. Dodd." " Your servant,
gentlemen." " Sir, we have one question to ask you."
" What is that, gentlemen?" " Why, we hear you have
preached a long time against the sin of drunkenness."
" I have, gentlemen." " Then, doctor, we have one
request you must and shall satisfy us in." " What is
that, gentlemen?" " Why, that you preach us a *sermon* from a *text* that we shall choose for you." " Ap-
point your time and place, gentlemen, and I will do it."
" The time is present, and the place is here, and that
hollow tree shall be your pulpit." " That's a compul-
sion, gentlemen; a man ought to have time to consider
what he is to preach." They insisted on a compliance,
or they would use him ill; not minding any expostu-
lations from the doctor, they accordingly forced him into
the *hollow tree.* The word they gave him for his *text*
was *malt!* from which he preached the following short,
but eloquent sermon.

THE SERMON.

My brethren, let me crave your reverend attention : I
am a little man, come at a short warning, to preach you

E 8

a short *sermon*, to a thin congregation, in an unworthy pulpit. Brethren, my text is *malt*: now I cannot divide it into *sentences*, because there are none; nor into *words*, it being but one; nor into *syllables*, it being but one also; therefore, I must, and necessity will oblige or rather force me to divide it into *letters*, which I find in my text to be four, M, A, L, T. M, my beloved, is *moral*, A *allegorical*, L *literal*, and T *theological*. Moral, my brethren, is well set forth to show and teach you drunkards good manners; wherefore, M my masters, A all of you, L listen, T to my *text*.

A, the allegorical, is when one thing is spoken of and another meant; the thing spoken of is *malt*, the thing meant is the *oil* of malt, or rather the spirit or strength of the *malt*, properly called *strong beer*; which you, gentlemen, make M your *meat*, A your *apparel*, L your *liberty*, and T your *treasure*. Now the literal is according to the letter, M *much*, A *ale*, L *little*, T *thirst*. Now the *theological* is according to the effects that it worketh, which I find in my text to be of two kinds: first, in this; secondly, in the *world* to come. Now the effects that I find it worketh in this world, are, in some M murder, in others A adultery, in all L looseness of life, and in many T treason. Now, the effects that I find it worketh in the world to come, are M misery, A anguish, L lamentation, and T torment. Now, my first use shall be a use of exhortation: M my masters, A all of you, L leave off, T tippling; or else M my masters, A all of you, L look for, T torment. Now, so much shall suffice for this explication; next only, by way of caution, take this for an inviolable truth, that a *drunkard* is the annoyance of *modesty*; the disturber of *civility*; a spoiler of *wealth*; the destroyer of *reason*; the brewer's *agent*; the ale house's *benefactor*; the *beggar's companion*; the *constable's perplexity*; his *wife's woe*; his *children's sorrow*; his *neighbour's scoff*; his *own shame*; and a *wilful madman*: by which he becomes a *true* and *lively* representation of a *walking swill-tub*, or a *tavern Bacchus*, in a monster of a man, by the picture of a *beast*. So, now, gentlemen, to conclude, I shall leave you, under the protection of the Almighty, to follow your own directions.

FAREWELL.

To say well and do well
    Ends with a letter;
To say well it is well,
    But do well is better:
Then take the best part
    Set down in this rhyme,
Consider it well,
    And act it in *time*.

"THEY ARE MINE."

A fellow of King's College, Cambridge, seated near an open window telling some bank-notes, was disconcerted by a breeze of wind suddenly blowing them out. He ran into the court in order to recover them, and, when below, looking up as they floated in the air, he espied the Provost looking down from an opposite window, upon which the disconsolate owner of the notes, in his anxiety, holding up his hands in a supplicating posture, exclaimed, *They are mine! They are mine!*"

" IBI SUNT CUNICULI."

Some students, *on a time*, went out shooting rabbits, and it so happened that they had one amongst their party who was unaccustomed to the sport. They gave him strict charge that he should not speak if he saw any game. After some time had elapsed, he espied some rabbits, and immediately bawled to his companions, " *Ibi sunt cuniculi !*" at which the game fled. Being reproved for disobeying orders, he answered, " Who the devil would have thought that rabbits understood Latin ?"

REFORMATION.

Judge Burnet, son of the famous Bishop of Salisbury, when young, is said to have been of a wild and dissipated turn. Being one day found by the bishop in a very serious humour, " What is the matter with you, Tom ?" said he, " what are you ruminating on ?" " A greater work than your lordship's History of the Reformation," answered the son. " Ay ! what is that ?" said the bishop?" " The *reformation of myself*, my lord," answered the son.

AN EXPEDIENT.

A Cantab, who had run up a reckoning at a house of entertainment some distance from Cambridge, having no money withal to discharge it, hit upon the following expedient. The host being present, he began to condemn

the wine, protesting it was execrably bad, observing—
" that his taste was delicate, as his father was a wine-
merchant; but, if the landlord would permit him to
look at the cask, he had a composition with him which
would make it better." The host consenting to try the
experiment, they accordingly repaired to the cellar, when
the Cantab bored a hole in the cask, and told the landlord to place his finger upon it, whilst he stepped up stairs
for the powder, which he said he had forgotten. The landlord, waiting a long time, and finding that the Cantab did
not come down, out of all patience, went up, and, lo ! his
guest had departed.

ELEGANT COMPLIMENT.

Mr. Henry Erskine, being one day in London, in company with the Duchess of Gordon, asked her, "Are we
never again to enjoy the honour and pleasure of your
grace's society at Edinburgh?" "Oh!" said her grace,
"Edinburgh is a vile dull place : I hate it." "Madam,"
replied the gallant barrister, "the sun might as well say,
there's a vile dark morning,—I won't rise to-day."

BACON.

A malefactor, under sentence of death, pretending
that he was related to him, on that account petitioned
Lord Chancellor Bacon for a *reprieve*. To which petition his lordship answered, "that he could not possibly
be *Bacon* till he had first been *hung*.

F 2

DOG LATIN.

On a time, two fellows of a college in Cambridge, riding together towards the Gog-Magog Hills, it chanced that a dog ran in the way of one of their horses: upon which the gentleman, to show that he had been a sportsman in his youth, calls out "*bellum equus.*" "Well done, old friend," cried his companion, I see you have not forgot your *dog-latin.*"

AN AWKWARD SITUATION.

A priest sitting with his companions, over his beer, at the door of a country alehouse, as in those days they did not scruple to do, upon some one mentioning the archbishop, who at the time was Cranmer, "That man," said the priest, "as great as he now is, was once but an ostler, and has no more learning than the goslings yonder on the green." Lord Essex, who was a great friend to Cranmer, hearing of it, despatched a messenger, and had him apprehended. Some months after, the archbishop, who was entirely ignorant of the affair, received a petition from the priest, full of penitence for his imprudence, and supplication for mercy. The primate sent for him, and inquired into the affair. "I hear," said he to the priest, "you have accused me of many things; amongst others, of being a very ignorant man. You have now an opportunity of setting your neighbours right in this matter, and may *examine* me, if you please." The priest, in great confusion, besought his grace to pardon him; and he never would offend in the same way again. "Well, then," says the archbishop, "since you will not examine me, let me examine you." The priest was thunderstruck, making many excuses, and owning he was not much learned in book-matters. The archbishop told him, he should not then go very deep; and asked him two or three of the plainest questions in the Bible : as— "Who was David's father? and who was Solomon's?" The priest, confused at his own ignorance, stood speechless. "You see (said the archbishop), how your accusation of me rises against yourself. You are an admirable judge of learning and learned men. Well, my friend, I had no hand in bringing you here, and have no desire to keep you.—Get home; and, if you are an ignorant man, learn at least to be an honest one."

PROPER DISTINCTION.

An under-graduate, invited by the peculiar beauty thereof, had unconsciously strayed into the garden of a certain D. D. then master of the college adjoining. He had not been there many minutes, when Dr. ——— entered himself, and, perceiving the student, in no very courteous manner he desired the young gentleman to walk out; which the under-graduate not doing (in the opinion of the doctor) in sufficient haste, the doctor demanded, rather peremptorily—"whether he knew who he was?"—at the same time informing the intruder he was Dr. ———. "That (replied the under-graduate) is impossible; for Dr. ——— is a *gentleman*, and you are a *blackg——d!*"

PORSON.

It is related of Porson, that his mode of communic
knowledge was truly amiable, and liberal in the ext
He would tell you all you wanted to know in a plai
direct manner, without any attempt to display his
riority, but merely to inform you; whereas, great
lars are apt to pride themselves on their brilliant
make a display of them, and leave you unenlighten

When he was invited to subscribe to the Shakesp
Papers, he excused himself by saying—"that he
scribed to no articles of faith."

He was fond of reading the Greek physicians,
when he lived in the Temple, slept with Galen und
head; not that Galen was his favourite, but becau
folio relieved his asthma.

The time to profit by Porson's learning was *inter i
dum*, for, as Chaucer says of the Sompnour,—

"And when that he well dronkin had with wine
    Then would he speke no word but Latine."

A WIFE LOST BY ABSENCE OF MINI

Harvest, early in life, was to have been married
daughter of Dr. Gibson, Bishop of London, but, fo
ting the day, he went out on a fishing-party. A
twelve o'clock he starts up, and exclaims, "Lord
me! I was to have been married to-day!" The l
however, found consolation by uniting herself to the
Bishop of Bristol; and poor Harvest remained a soli
bachelor.

OXFORD VERSUS CAMBRIDGE.

In 1532, two "pert Oxonians" took a journey to Cambridge, and in the public schools challenged any to dispute with them on the following questions:—

An jus civile sit medicinâ præstantius?

In English, as much as to say,—What does most execution, civil law or medicine?—A nice point to decide. The other question, which formed the subject of serious argumentation, was the following.—

An mulier condemnata, bis ruptis laqueis, sit tertio suspendenda?

Ridley, afterwards bishop of that name, was one of the opponents on this interesting occasion; who administered the *flagella linguæ* to one of those pert pretenders to logic lore with such happy effect, that the other was afraid to set his wit upon him.

PALEY'S SKETCH OF HIS EARLY ACADEMICAL LIFE.

In the year 1795, during one of his visits to Cambridge, Dr. Paley, in the course of a conversation on the subject, gave the following account of the early part of his own academical life; and it is here given, on the authority and in the very words of a gentleman who was present at the time, as a striking instance of the peculiar frankness with which he was in the habit of relating the adventures of his youth. "I spent (says Paley) the two first years of my under-graduateship happily, but unprofitably. I was constantly in society, where we were not immoral, but idle and rather expensive. At the commencement of my third year, however, after having left the usual party at rather a late hour in the evening, I was awakened at five in the morning by one of my companions, who stood at my bed-side and said—'Paley, I have been thinking what a d—d fool you are. I could do nothing, probably, were I to try, and can afford the life I lead: you could do everything, and cannot afford it. I have had no sleep during the whole night on account of these reflections, and am now come solemnly to inform you, that, if you persist in your indolence, I must renounce your society.' I was so struck (continued Dr. Paley), with the visit and the visitor, that I lay in bed great part of the day, and formed my plan: I ordered my bed-maker to prepare my fire every evening, in order that it might be lighted by myself; I arose at five, read during the whole of the day, except such hours as chapel and hall required, allotting to each portion of time its peculiar branch of study; and, just before the closing of gates (nine o'clock), I went to a neighbouring coffee-house, where I constantly regaled upon a mutton-chop and a dose of milk-punch: and thus, on taking my bachelor's degree, I became *Senior Wrangler*."

FEAR CURED.

The poet Gray was remarkably fearful of *fire*; and, that he might be prepared to meet any sudden danger arising from such a calamity, he always kept a ladder of ropes in his room. He used occasionally to exercise himself by *descending* and *ascending*, with a view to become expert in case of real necessity. This attracted the attention of some of his more mischievous brother collegians, who determined to attempt a cure of this habit. Accordingly, in the dead of a very dark night, they roused him from his bed with a cry of fire! taking care to inform him the staircase was in a flame. Up went the window in an instant, and Gray hastened down his ladder with no slight velocity, into a *tub of water* which had been previously prepared to receive him. The joke operated as a cure on Gray; however, he would not forgive it, but immediately changed his college.

BETTER ACQUAINTED.

Dr. Howard, when rector of St. George, Southwark, went round with the parish officers collecting a brief. Among the rest, they called on a grocer with whom the doctor had a running account; and, to prevent being asked for a settlement, the doctor inquired if he was not some trifle in his debt? On referring to the ledger, there appeared a balance of *seventeen shillings*, against the doctor, who had recourse to his pocket, and, pulling out some *halfpence*, a little *silver*, and a *guinea*, the grocer, eyeing the latter with a little surprise, being well acquainted with the doctor's poverty, exclaimed— "Good God, sir, you have got a stranger there!" "Indeed I have, Mr. Browne," replied the wit, at the same time returning it very deliberately to his pocket,—"*and, before we part, we will be better acquainted!*"

BAD LANGUAGE.

Sir John Robinson spoke bad *French*, and the King of Denmark worse *English*. Some hours after the king and Sir John had been together, Lord Chesterfield entered, and with a very grave face condoled with Sir John on the misunderstanding between him and the king. The astonished knight protested there was no truth whatever in the report: which Lord Chesterfield interrupted by saying, "Confess or deny, Sir John, as you please ; but every one knows there was much bad language between you."

TOM RANDOLPH

Was a man of such pregnant wit, that the Muses may seem not only to have smiled, but to have tickled at his nativity. Once on a day, as it often happens in drinking, a quarrel arose between Randolph and another gentleman, which grew so high, that the gentleman drew his sword, and, striking at Randolph, cut off his little finger ; whereupon, in an extempore humour, Randolph instantly made the following verses : —

" Arithmetic nine digits and no more
   Admits of, then I have all my store ;
   But what mischance have ta'en from my left-hand,
   It seems did only for a *cipher* stand ;
   Hence, when I scan my verse, if I do miss,
   I will impute the fault only to this :
   A finger's loss, I speak it not in sport,
   Will make a verse a foot too short."

THE RETORT.

In the year 1712, Matthew Prior, who was then a fellow of St. John's College, Cambridge, and who, not long before, had been employed by Queen Anne as her plenipotentiary at the court of France, came to Cambridge, and the next morning paid a visit to the master of his college (then Dr. Gower, or Jenkins). The master was attached to Prior's principles, had a great opinion of his abilities, and a great respect for his character in the world; but he had a much greater opinion and respect for himself. He knew his own dignity too well to permit a fellow of his college to sit down in his presence; and therefore kept his seat himself, and let the queen's ambassador stand. A little piqued at his reception, Matthew Prior, who was not then noted as a *dab* at an epigram, thought the present too tempting an opportunity to be let slip. He therefore, on his way to the Rose, from his college, where he went to dine, composed the following epigram, which he addressed to the master :—

EPIGRAM.

" I *stood*, sir, patient at your feet,
　　Before your elbow-chair;
But make a bishop's throne your seat,
　　I'll kneel before you there.

One only thing can keep you down,
　　For your great soul too mean;
You'd not, to mount a bishop's throne,
　　Pay *homage* to the *queen*."

TRAIT OF PORSON.

The same spirit of independence, so strongly discernible in Porson's moral character, was also visible in his literary character; and he never appeared so sore, or so irritable, as when a Wakefield or a Hermann offered to set him right, or hold their tapers to light him on his way. He considered them, and others, on such occasions, as four-footed animals; and used to say that, in future, whatever he wrote, he would take care they should not reach it with their paws, though they stood on their hind legs to get at it.

IMPROMPTU.

In a mathematical examination at Benét, in Corpus-Christi College, Cambridge, a student, being required to define a *triangle and a circle*, made the following *impromptu*:—

" Let mathematicians and geometricians
    Talk of *circles'* and *triangles'* charms;
  But the figure I prize is a *girl* with bright eyes,
    And the *circle* that's formed by her arms."

ELEGANT RETORT.

BY THE LATE LORD ELLENBOROUGH.

Lord Ellenborough, who was educated at St. John's College, Cambridge, when Mr. Law, was so unfortunate as to make an enemy in the person of Lord Kenyon, who took every opportunity of annoying him, and repressing his rising talents. In a cause where Mr. afterwards Lord Erskine was engaged as counsel on the opposite side, and who made a violent speech, containing some personalities which Mr. Law was obliged to notice, this conduct of the judge drew from Mr. Law, when he rose to reply, the following *elegant retort*, out of Virgil :—

> " Dicta ferox non me tua fervida terrent
> Dii me terrent et Jupiter hostis."

" HOW D'YE DO, OLD CODGER?"

An undergraduate, soon after he had commenced residence in the University of Cambridge, and whilst he was distinguished by the appellation of *freshman*, thinking to *come it strong*, started one morning upon his nag for a breathing towards the *Gog-Magog Hills!* Seeing an old gentleman jogging along upon his *black charger*, he determined to join him for a *quiz*, and, riding along side his man, he began with—" *How d'ye do, Old Codger?*" His companion, nothing abashed, answered very coolly—" *Pretty well, Young Codger!*" Finding he had mistaken his man, after a few more attempts at a *quiz*, which were retorted by his companion, who was no novice at such sport, the collegian put his nag into a round pace, and left his companion far behind. The Cantab having reached his college, he soon after joined some of his companions (who happened to be men of longer standing than himself), to whom he related his adventures; at the same time describing the *Old Codger.* From the description he gave, no doubt was enter-

tained by them, but that the *Old Codger* was a certain
D. D., who was then Vice-Chancellor. This information put the *freshman* in a *funk*, particularly when they
added, that he would undoubtedly be *convened*, and, perhaps, *rusticated*, for his insolence. Some few hours
after, whilst he with the rest were over a bottle, a note
was brought to our hero, requiring his attendance on
Mr. Vice-Chancellor, to account for his impertinence in
the morning. His friends expressed their concern, but
recommended his going immediately. Agreeably to
this advice, he set off for the doctor's residence, and,
knocking at his door, was desired to come in. He immediately began by apologizing, and presenting the
note he had received; but, on Mr. Vice-Chancellor
saying he knew nothing of the summons, he found, to
his no small chagrin, that the whole was a *hoax*.

DELIGHTS OF GERMAN TRAVELLING.

The erudite John Tweddell, Esq. whose remains lie
mouldering in the bosom of his parent earth, at Athens,
in the *Temple of Theseus* (the mysterious and ever to be
lamented disappearance of whose *Researches* still remains
to be accounted for), was at his death a fellow of Trinity
College, Cambridge. Speaking of German travelling,
in one of his letters to a friend, A. D. 1796, he says :—
" Our carriage is in complete condition still, and that
is saying a great deal. Mr. Webb's was broken to
pieces in the same roads—such roads ! such inns ! and
such beds ! I slept once or twice upon straw in preference ; and, after all, upon combing my head, I found
that I had *increased my family*—but this was not the

effect of *being in the straw.*" In another letter, to a lady about to travel, he writes on the same subject :— " You must make up your minds to bad accommodations, frauds, stoppages, &c.—I would have added, and dirty sheets, if I did not presume that you would have the precaution to take your own. Two pair will be sufficient, or even one, for there will be sufficient time to *wash* them while you change horses—there's comfort for you. You must take a provision of *small-toothed combs* with you—your head will soon tell you why. Another thing which you must take with you is *patience*—you will want it at every inn. You will find 'the *first* horses yoked a hundred yards before the second horses : you may think that the reason of this is, in order to go before, for the purpose of ordering *dinner ;* but it is not so."

TIT FOR TAT.

During the administration of the famous Lord Chatham, who was educated at Trinity College, Cambridge, Dr. Markham, Archbishop of York, delivered a charge to his clergy, reflecting highly on the administration of the noble lord. It so happened, that the poet Mason preached a visitation sermon before the archbishop, in the Cathedral Church of York, soon after. Mason, who differed entirely with the archbishop in politics, facetiously chose the following text on the occasion :—" Yet Michael the archangel, when contending with the *devil* he disputed about the body of Moses, durst not bring against him a railing accusation, but said, the Lord rebuke thee." *Jude* 9.

Soon after the preaching of this sermon, by Mason,

some one was declaiming in the House of Lords against the clergy interfering in *politics*, and during whose speech Lord Chatham came into the house; but, not knowing what had passed at York, he leaned over a noble duke, lately deceased, and asked to what the speaker was alluding. On being informed, his lordship attacked the archbishop most eloquently, and so ably retaliated for the past, that the archbishop, wanting temper naturally, was disabled from replying with any coherence.

ETERNITY OF HELL TORMENTS.

Soon after the appointment of Mr. Jebb, fellow of Peterhouse, and Mr. Watson, afterwards Bishop of Landaff, to the office of *Moderators* for the first time, they sent Paley, then in his third year (the time at which every under-graduate who contends for mathematical honours does the same thing), an *act* to *keep* in the schools. Paley was prepared with the mathematical question, and, referring to *Johnson's Questiones Philosophicæ*, a book then common in the University, in which the subject usually disputed in the *schools*, and the names of the authors who had written on each side, were contained, he fixed upon two others, as not having been proposed for *disputation*, to his knowledge, before: the one against *capital punishments*,—the other against the *eternity of hell torments*. As soon as it was rumoured amongst the heads of colleges, that Paley, who was then young, and whose abilities were well known, had proposed such questions, the master of his college was desired to interfere and put a stop to it. Dr. Thomas consequently summoned him to the lodge, and objected, in strong terms, to both his questions, but insisted upon his relinguishing the *last*. Paley immediately went to the *Moderator*, and acquainted him with this peremptory command. Mr. Watson was indignant that " the heads of colleges should interfere in a matter which belonged solely (as he said) to him, for he was the judge of the propriety or impropriety of the *questions* sent to him." " Are you, sir," continued Watson, " independent of your college ! If you are not, *these* shall be the questions for your *act*." Paley replied, " that he should be sorry to offend the college; and therefore wished to change the last question." " Very well," replied the Moderator, " the best way, then, to satisfy the scruples of these gentlemen will be for you to *defend* the *Eternity of Hell Torments :*"—and, changing his *thesis* to the *affirmative*, he actually did so.

MATTHEW MATTOCKS.

A gentleman, who had just taken his degree of B. A. in the University of Cambridge, going down into the north of England on a visit immediately after, was asked by a person (whose pronunciation savoured of the provincial), " whether he knew

MATHEMATICS."

The Cantab, supposing that he alluded to a person of that name who lived in the neighbourhood, replied—" I don't know *Matthew Mattocks*, but I know his brother *Richard*."

G

DOCTOR GLYNN'S RECEIPT FOR DRESSING A CUCUMBER.

Dr. Glynn, whose name will long be remembered in Cambridge, was one of those beings who would occasionally unstring the bow, lest it should lose its elasticity. Being one day in attendance on a lady in the quality of her physician, he took the liberty of lecturing her on the impropriety of her eating *cucumber*, of which she was immoderately fond; and gave her the following humorous receipt for dressing them:—"Peel the cucumber," said the doctor, " with great care; then cut it into very thin slices, pepper and salt it well, and then— *throw it away!*"

EXTEMPORANEOUS VERSES.

The following extemporaneous effusion was poured forth by a gentleman of Benét, or Corpus Christi College, Cambridge :—

Have you not heard the cock's loud crowing
    Ere the day began to dawn?
Have you not heard the cattle lowing,
    And the huntsman's sounding horn?

Have you not heard the church bells ringing,
    For some happy wedded pair?
Have you not heard the skylark singing,
    Soaring in the limpid air?

Have you not heard the tempest roar,
    Driving on the pelting rain?
If you have heard all these, and more,
    Perhaps——you'll hear them all again!

PORSON'S POLITICS.

They never interrupted an harmonious intercour
with him, who pays this tribute to his memory, and
whom, in a moment of confidence, he gave, in his ow
hand-writing, a pamphlet, written in answer to M
Burke's Reflections on the French Revolution. It
termed—"*A New Catechism for the Natives of Ham*
shire." The humour of the *tract* consists in playir
upon the expression, "*swinish multitude*," said to ha
been applied to the common people by Mr. Burk
The following is the beginning and ending of the—

TRACT.

Question. What is your name?
Answer. Hog or Swine.
Q. Did God make you a *hog?*
A. No; God made me *man* in his own image: th
right honourable *Sublime and Beautiful* made me a *swir*
Q. How did he make you a *swine?*
A. By muttering obscure and uncouth spells. He
a dealer in the *black art.*
Q. Who feeds you?
A. Our *drivers*, the only real men in this country.
Q. How many hogs are you in all?
A. Seven or eight millions.
Q. How many *drivers?*
A. Two or three thousand.
Q. With what do they feed you?
A. Generally with husks, swill, draff, malt, grain
and now and then with a little barley-meal and a few pc
tatoes; and, when they have too much butter-milk them
selves, they give us some.

G 2

The following must be allowed not to be destitute of humour:—

Q. What are the *interpreters** called ?

A. The black-letter sisterhood.

Q. Why do they give the office to women ?

A. Because they have a fluent tongue and a knack of scolding.

Q. How are they dressed?

A. In gowns and false hair.

Q. What are the principal orders?

A. Three : *writers, talkers,* and *hearers;* which last are also called *deciders.*

Q. What is their general business ?

A. To discuss the mutual quarrels of the *hogs,* and to punish their affronts to any or all of their drivers.

Q. If two hogs quarrel, how do they apply to the sisterhood ?

A. Each hog goes separately to a *writer.*

Q. What does the *writer ?*

A. She goes to a *talker.*

Q. What does the talker ?

A. She goes to a *hearer,* or *decider.*

Q. What does the hearer decide ?

A. What she pleases.

Q. If a hog be decided to be in the right, what is the *consequence ?*

A He is almost *ruined.*

Q. If in the wrong, what ?

A. He is *quite ruined.*

After some facetious remarks on the clergy, who are termed peace-makers, the dialogue proceeds :—

* Judges.

Q. How are these peace-makers rewarded ?

A. With *potatoes.*

Q. What, all ?

A. Ten per cent. only.

Q. Then you have still *ninety* left in the hundred ?

A. No ; we have only *forty* left.

Q. What becomes of the odd *fifty ?*

A. The drivers take them, partly for a small recompense for protecting us, and partly to make money o them, for the prosecution of law-suits with the neighbouring farmers.

Q. You talk sensibly for a hog ; where had you you information ?

A. From a very *learned pig.*

The following is given by way of answer to the question—by what ceremony the *hog* is disenchanted, and resumes his natural shape :—

A. The *hog* is going to be disenchanted, grovels before the chief driver, who holds an iron skewer over him and gives him a smart blow on the shoulder, to remind him at once of his former subjection and future submission. Immediately he starts up, like the devil from *Ithuriel's* spear, in his proper shape, and ever after goes about with a nickname. He then beats his hogs without mercy, and, when they implore his compassion, and beg him to recollect he was once their *fellow-swine,* he denies that ever he was a *hog.*

This curious dialogue thus concludes :—

Q. What is the general wish of the *hogs* at present ?

A. To save their *bacon.*

Chorus of Hogs.

Amen !

STEALING.

A Johnian, now deceased, one day met a Trinity man, walking under the *piazza* of Neville's Court, of whom he had some knowledge. Going suddenly up to the Trinitarian, he addressed him with,—" Sir, you are a thief!" The Trinitarian, all astonishment at the tone in which the accusation was made, demanded an explanation. " Sir," answered the Johnian, smiling, " *You steal from the sun.*"

THE CANONICAL WIG.

It so happened one day, that Doctor Howard passed by the shop of a peruke-maker, when his pocket, which was too often the case, overflowed with emptiness. He saw a *canonical wig* in the window, which took his fancy very much, and, in order to obtain credit, he informed the master of the shop he was rector of St. George's Southwark, and chaplain to the Princess Dowager of Wales. Happy in the acquisition of such a customer, the hair-dresser, who had received the doctor's order to that effect, finished a wig with the utmost despatch; but before he sent it home, he heard some whispers about the reverend doctor, which did not perfectly please him, and he therefore ordered his journeyman, whom he sent with the wig, not to deliver it without the money. " I have brought your wig, sir," said the barber, when ushered into the doctor's presence. " Very well," said his reverence, " put it down." " I can't, sir," replied the barber, " without the *cash.*" The doctor, who was just then very low in the pocket, and anxious to possess the wig, said—" Let me try whether it will fit me?"

This was so reasonable a request, that the barber readily consented, and the doctor had no sooner put it on his head, than he ordered the poor barber out of the room, giving him to understand that, since it was sold to him it was now become his property.

DO ILL.

At a party in Cambridge, where the merits of a certain *belle* happened to be discussed, two Cantabs, who had some knowledge of the lady, took opposite sides, and contended very warmly for each other's opinion ; indeed so high did the question run, that they became quite clamorous on the subject. Upon which, a lady of the party jocosely observed, " that she feared they would be obliged to end the affair by fighting a duel ! " " In that case, madam," replied one of the Cantabs, " we should *do ill !* "

PRINCIPAL AND INTEREST.

It is related of the celebrated Burke, that he sent his son to St. John's College, Cambridge, to complete his studies ; and, after the young gentleman had resided there some time, the *bills* were of course sent to him by the tutor for payment. Burke suffered them to remain unpaid, nor did he take any notice of the circumstance. The tutor, at length, grown tired of waiting payment, wrote to request, that, if it was not convenient for Mr. Burke to pay the *principal*, he would pay the *interest*. To this reasonable request Burke laconically answered ;—" Since it is neither my *principle* to pay the *interest*, nor my *interest* to pay the *principal*."

LAPSUS LINGUÆ.

When Paley was installed as sub-dean, in the Cathedral of Lincoln, 1795, he proceeded from thence to take his degree of D. D. in Cambridge. He preached his *Concio ad Clerum* in February, and on that occasion, as he was no poet, and little skilled in Latin prosody, he unfortunately pronounced the word *profugus, profūgus.* This blunder of Paley's gave rise to the following epigram from one of the University wits :—

EPIGRAM.

"Italiam, fato *profugus*, lavinaque venit
  Litora ;
  Errat Virgilius forte *profūgus* erat."

DR. JORTIN,

Who was of Jesus College, Cambridge, was once asked by a friend, why he did not publish his sermons.—"They shall sleep," answered the doctor, "til I sleep."

ABSENCE OF MIND.

The effect of absence of mind is well exemplified in an incident which happened some time since to a well-known gentleman of Magdalen College, Cambridge. He had taken his *watch* from his pocket to mark the time he intended to boil an egg for his breakfast, when a friend, en-

tering his room, found him absorbed in some abstrus
calculation, with the *egg* in his hand, upon which he wa
looking intently, and the *watch* supplying its place in th
saucepan of boiling water.

FLYING TO THE UTMOST BOUNDS OF INFI NITE SPACE.

During the days of Bishop Hinchley, at a visitatior
sermon, preached before the University of Cambridge,
the preacher indulged himself in much speculative argumentation, and concluded by speaking, though rheto-
rically, by no means mathematically or metaphysically
of an *angel's flying to the utmost bounds of infinite space.*

DELICACY.

Dr. Jortin was, by some writer, once accused of *indeli-
cacy*. All the world laughed at the conceit, and Jortin himself was surprised into a *grin*. "How comes it, John," said
a friend of his, "that you should have the reputation of
less delicacy than the broker?" "I'll tell you," said the
doctor. "Rambling one day in the environs of the zo-
diac, instead of making my bow and my speech, I happened to turn my posteriors upon *Ursa Major!*"

KILLING TIME.

Paley frequently mixed in card-parties, and was considered a skilful player at whist; but he would, at all
times, readily forego the amusement for conversation with

an intelligent companion: A lady once observed to him at a card-table—"that the only excuse for their playing was, that it served to kill time." "The best defence possible, madam," replied he, "though *time* will in the end kill us!"

COMPLIMENTS.

Mr. Yates, the celebrated master of the free grammar-school at Appleby, which he had taught with credit and success for half a century, when in his eightieth year, still retaining the vigour of his faculties, became intimate with Paley. Many of their mutual compliments are remembered by their intimate friends; amongst others, the following:—"Mr. Paley reasons like Locke," was the observation of Yates; "Mr. Yates writes like Erasmus," was the equally merited reply of Paley.

FACETIOUS SKETCH OF THE CHARACTER OF PAUL I. OF RUSSIA.

Tweddall, in a letter to one of his friends, dated Moscow, 1797, thus facetiously describes the character of *Paul I.*:—"He is," says Tweddell, "a great imitator of Frederic II., for which reason he wears great boots and hideous uniforms, and exercises his troops at six o'clock in the morning without his hat on, when the cold is at sixteen degrees. He wishes to unite magnificence with economy—for which reason he makes superb presents to individuals, and great retrenchments in the general departments of state. He certainly has the most

brilliant court in Europe; it is truly splendid. On th
day of his *coronation*, at dinner, the lieutenant-colonel
presented his dishes upon one knee. How can this east
ern despot pretend to unite such base servitude with hi
love of the military? He is capricious and minute—at
taching weight to trifles. All the military are obliged t
have long *queues*; a man with short hair cannot command
his armies. General *Mack* would not have sufficien
merit to be a *sergeant*, for he has the vice of *baldness*: th
emperor would treat him as the naughty boys treated
Elisha. He judges all men upon the model of *Samson*
and conceives their force to be in their *hair*. His firs
acts, such as the liberation of *Koskiusko*, placed him in
fair light, and made him appear brighter than he ough
to appear. In short, *Paul* is a poor thing; he does no
want sense, but he has not capacity to embrace a com
prehensive system of measures. He is a little mar
standing on tip-toe; he *libels* dignity when he struts
and reminds me of a poultry-yard, when he traverses th
palace in the midst of the dames of honour.

FULLER ALL OVER.

The Rev. Thomas Fuller, who was educated a
Queen's College, Cambridge, was in his day a great *pun
ster*, and, also, a man of most lively wit. He was ex
tremely corpulent, and one day, as he was riding in com
pany with a gentleman of his acquaintance, named
Sparrowhawk, he could not resist the opportunity of pass
ing a joke upon him. "Pray what is the difference,"
said Fuller, between an *owl* and a *sparrowhawk*?" "Oh,"
retorted the other, sarcastically, "an owl is *fuller* in th
head, *fuller* in the body, and *fuller* all over!"

KEEPING A CONSCIENCE.

The great *controversy* on the propriety of requiring a subscription to *articles of faith*, as practised by the church of England, excited at this time (1772) a very strong sensation amongst the members of the two universities.   At Oxford the high church were completely triumphant; but in Cambridge the discussion ran high, and exercised talents and ingenuity on both sides of the question, attended with no small asperity Paley was personally attached to many of the reforming party, but, though favourable to their claims, he did not sign the clerical petition which was presented to the House of Commons for relief; alleging jocularly to Mr. Jebb, as an apology for his refusal, that, " he could not afford to keep a conscience."

RETORT ON RETORT.

Dr. South, in his "Animadversions on Dr. Sherlock' Vindication of the Trinity," in 1693, occasionally reflected upon Archbishop Tillotson, for his " signal and peculiar encomium, as he calls it, on the reasoning abilities of the Socinians;" and, being desirous of knowing the archbishop's opinion of his performance, procured a friend of his to draw it from him, who gave i to this effect,—that the doctor wrote like a man, but bit like a dog.   This being reported to Dr. South, he answered, that " he had rather bite like a dog, than fawn like one."   To which the archbishop replied, that " for his part, he should choose to be a *spaniel* rather than a *cur*.

A DELICATE MORSEL.

A son of Grantor, whose delight was rather in the sports of the field than in strutting about the streets of the University *à la Cantab*, had been out very early one morning at a fox-chase : from which returning at a late hour, his appetite became so excessively keen, that it was not to be resisted, and accordingly he resolved to beg alms at the first farmhouse he might light on. His sight rendered keener by the cravings of his stomach, he soon espied a small house at some distance, which having gained, he offered his humble petition to mine hostess. The old dame courtesied, begged our hero would alight, and regretted she had no better cheer to offer him than the remnant of a *meat pie*, the remains of their own frugal meal. " Anything is better than nothing," cried the Cantab, at the same time entreating she would not delay a moment in placing it before him ; for he already devoured it in imagination, so keen was his hunger. " Here it is," said the dame, producing it at the same instant from a small cupboard near the elbow of our sportsman, who turned round as she spoke—" Here it is, sir ; it is only made of the *odds* and *ends*, but may hope your honour would like it, though it has mutton and beef and all that in it." " Charming ! my good woman, it needs no apology ; I never tasted a more delicious morsel in my life !" continued the Cantab, as he swallowed or rather devoured mouthful after mouthful. " But there is *fish* in it, too," said he, as he greedily sucked what he supposed to be a bone. " Fish," exclaimed the old dame, looking intently on what the sportsman had got in his hand : " fish, nae, sir,—why lack a day (cried she) ! if that beant our Billy's *comb !*"

OVER-WISE.

In a lecture-room of St. John's College, Cambridge, a student one morning, construing or translating some part of a Greek tragedy (the Madea of Euripides), came to the following passage—

$$A\lambda\lambda' \; ouk \; \alpha\varrho\iota\sigma o\varphi o\varsigma \; \epsilon\iota\mu\iota.$$

To which he gave the proper sense—

"I am not *over-wise*."

but pausing as if he doubted its correctness—"You are quite right, sir," observed the humorous lecturer; "go on."

TRUTH AND RHYME.

In the days of Charles II., candidates for holy orders were expected to respond in Latin, to the various interrogatories put to them by the bishop or his examining chaplain. When the celebrated Dr. Isaac Barrow (who was fellow of Trinity College, and tutor to the immortal Newton) had taken his bachelor's degree, and disengaged himself from collegiate leading-strings, he presented himself before the bishop's chaplain who, with the stiff stern visage of the times, said to Barrow—

"*Quid est fides?*" (what is faith?)
"*Quod non vides*" (what thou dost not see),

answered Barrow with the utmost promptitude. The chaplain, a little vexed at Barrow's laconic answer,—

continued—" *Quid est spes?*" (what is hope?)
" *Magna res*" (a great thing),
replied the young candidate in the same breath.
" *Quid est charitas?*" (what is charity?)
was the next question.
" *Magna raritas*" (a great rarity),
was again the prompt reply of Barrow, blending truth
and rhyme with a precision that staggered the reverend
examiner; who went direct to the bishop and told him,
that a young Cantab, of *philosophic mien* (the faces of
reading men in those days being generally in the like-
ness of *inverted* isosceles triangles), had thought proper
to give rhyming answers to three several moral questions:
and added, that he believed his name was Barrow, of
Trinity College, Cambridge. "Barrow, Barrow!" said
the bishop, who well knew the literary and moral worth
of the young Cantab, " if that's the case, ask him no
more questions : for he is much better qualified," continued his lordship, " to examine us than we him." Barrow received his letters of orders forthwith.

TRUTH *versus* POLITENESS.

At a tea-party, where some Cantabs happened to be
present, after the first dish had been handed round, the
lady, who was presiding over the tea equipage, " hoped
the tea was good." " Very good indeed, madam," was
the general reply, till it came to the turn of one of the
Cantabs to speak, who, between truth and politeness,
shrewdly observed—" That the *tea* was *excellent*, but
the *water* was *smoky!*"

PRESENCE OF MIND.

The arm of Dr. Barrow, like his argument, was powerful, as the following instance of his prowess, humanity, and love of reasoning, as related by his biographer, will show. Being on a visit to a friend in the country, he rose before daybreak one morning, and went into the yard. He had scarcely left the door, when a large English mastiff, left loose to guard the premises during the night, sprung upon him. Barrow grappled with the dog, threw him on the ground, and himself upon him. In this position he remained, till one of the servants made his appearance, who instantly called off the dog, and extricated the doctor from his perilous situation. "Why didn't you strangle him, doctor?" asked the man. "Because," answered Barrow, "the brute was only doing his duty: and I thought within myself, as I kept him under me, if we all did the same, how much happier the community would be."

A FAREWELL SCENE.

Christopher Anstey, who was bred at King's College, and well known in the world as the author of the " *New Bath Guide*," and an elegant version of *Gay's Fables*, was, during his residence in the University of Cambridge, extremely irregular in his conduct. For something which was deemed a serious breach of the college rules, he was required to make an apology to the heads of the society to which he belonged : he accordingly appeared before the parties at the appointed time, but, instead of apologizing, he aggravated his offence, by making several observations, which were deemed inso-lent and impertinent. He was now threatened with *rustication*, forfeiture of collegiate *honours*, &c. unless he offered a very serious apology ; for which purpose he was *convened* before the whole college on a day named Anstey entered the combination-room (where sat the doctors, masters of arts, bachelors, and others of his college), amidst a profound silence, and, with hypocritic phiz and affected contrition, he proceeded to address the dignitaries of Granta. Turning towards the doctors, he thus began—" *Valete, doctores sine doctrinâ!*" (Farewell, ye doctors without learning !) Then to the masters of arts, he continued,—" *Valete, magistri sine artibus!*" (Farewell, ye masters without arts!) Lastly, facing the bachelors, he exclaimed—" *Denique valete, baccalaurei digniores baculo!*" (At length farewell, ye bachelors worthy of a thrashing !) So saying, with a sarcastic in-clination of the head, he walked out. It is needless to add, he was despoiled of his honours, degraded, and expelled. To the unfortunate conclusion of this affair, he alludes in the following couplet of his " *Bath Guide:*"

" On the margin of Cam, where, studious of ease,
 I spent seven long years, and then lost my degrees."

READY REPLY.

It is generally known that the grass-plots in the col-lege courts, or quadrangles, as they are called in Oxford, are not for the unhallowed feet of the undergraduates ; indeed, it is, in one college in Cambridge, a fine of *two*

H

and *sixpence*, for any man of the college *in statu pupillar*
to pollute them : but these regulations are rather intended to preserve the turf, than for distinction.   Some
however, are hardy enough to venture in despite of all
remonstrance.   The late Bishop of Bristol, then master
of Trinity, had often observed a student of his college
invariably to cross the green, when, in obedience to the
calls of his appetite, he went to hall to dine.   One day
the bishop determined to reprove the delinquent for
invading the rights of his superiors, and for that purpose he threw up the sash at which he was sitting
and called to the student—" Sir, I never look out of my
window, but I see you walking across the grass-plot."
" My lord," replied the offender instantly, " I never
walk across the grass-plot, but I see you looking out of
your window."   The prelate, who well knew how to
appreciate a retort, pleased at the readiness of the reply,
closed his window, convulsed with laughter.

NOT *versus* NOTT.

A gentleman of Maudlin, whose name was *Nott*, happening one evening to be out, was returning late from
his friend's rooms in rather a merry mode, and, withal,
not quite able to preserve his centre of gravity.   In his
way he attracted the attention of the proctor, who demanded his name and college.   " I am *Nott* of Maudlin" was the reply, hiccupping.   " Sir," said the proctor,
in an angry tone, " I did not ask of what college you are
not, but of what college you are."   " I am *Nott* of
Maudlin," was again the broken reply.   The proctor,
enraged at what he considered contumely, insisted on

accompanying him to Maudlin, whither having arrived, he demanded of the porter, " whether he knew the gentleman."—" Know him, sir," said the porter, " yes, it is Mr. *Nott*, of this college." The proctor now perceived his error in *not* understanding the gentleman, and, laughing heartily at the affair, wished him a good night.

A VERY CUTTING RETORT.

Archbishop Tillotson had, by some means, incurred the displeasure of Sir John Trevor, who had been ex-pelled the House of Commons for several misdemeanors. Sir John, one day meeting Tillotson, cried out, " I hate to see an *Atheist* in the shape of a churchman."—" And I," replied the archbishop, " hate to see a *knave* in any shape."

THE BLUE BOAR.

In olden times, the students of the different colleges in Cambridge obtained various *nicknames*; but why or wherefore are questions few persons are qualified to answer generally. For instance, the men of Trinity College are called *bull-dogs*; Maudlin men, *rats*; Clarehall men, *greyhounds*, &c.; and since the men of St. John's College obtained the name of *hogs*, it is no very uncommon thing for men of other colleges to say, when they see a pig—" *There goes a Johnian.*" It is necessary to inform some of our readers, that the gown-men of Trinity wear *blue gowns*, but the *toga* worn by a *Johnian* is *black*. It happened on a day, that a *Trinitarian*, brimful of wine, was passing by the sign of the *Blue Boar* (which hung nearly opposite his own college, and had been newly painted and richly gilt), with his spirits raised to the (Nth +1), when the *sign* attracted his attention, and, nimbly climbing the post from which it hung suspended, he in an instant wrenched it from the hinges and dashed it to the ground, exclaiming,—" D—— me, if a *Johnian* shall wear a *blue gown !*"

BILLET FOR BILLET.

One of the tutors of Queen's College, Cambridge, was much annoyed one day, when dining in hall, by the loquacity of an undergraduate, who sat at an opposite table to himself; indeed, so much so, that flesh and blood could bear it no longer; and, calling one of the *gyps*, who was waiting at table, he wrote with his pencil, on a slip of paper, the following elegant reproof:—

" *Vir sapit qui pauca loquitur.*"

(A wise man talks little.)   The undergraduate, without hesitation, turned over the paper, and wrote on the blank side,—

" *Vir loquitur qui pauca sapit,*"

(The man talks who is a little wise), and returned the paper to the tutor by the same hands that brought it.

UNCONSCIOUS VANITY.

It is said by a writer of no small credit in the literary horizon, " *that a man's sense of his own superiority may beget a degree of pardonable vanity.*"   This has been truly exemplified in the person of a gentleman holding an official situation in the University of Cambridge. It is related, that when he was examined for his degree of B. A. in the Senate House, he did not succeed very well at first; but on the last day he challenged the whole of those above him, and, although he was far below, he beat the whole, and was declared *Senior Wrangler*, or worthy of the first mathematical honours of his year. This circumstance caused him to be particularly noticed, and, being of rather a bashful turn, he imagined persons to be observing him, when, in fact, their attention was directed to other objects. The following is a remarkable instance of this kind. He went to London soon after his success, and, during his stay, he one night visited one of the large theatres. It so happened, that his late Majesty, George the Third, entered the theatre at the same instant with our hero, and of course the whole audience rose; our *Senior Wrangler*, imagining the honour to be intended for himself, all abashed, exclaimed, " *This is too much!*"

DEAFNESS, FEAR, AND IMAGINATION.

The Rev. Mr. D——, of Trinity College, Cambridge, ing his residence, as well known to dean, porter, and cook, of that splendid and royal foundation, by his irregularities and epicureanism, as to the literary world by his amusing and scientific publications, fell into the river Cam, on a raw and gusty day in December, as he was displaying his skill in skaiting; an exercise in which he had attained such skill and proficiency, that *Hal Broeck*, at the Hague, who could cut his own name in *German text*, on the ice, could scarcely have competed with him

The effect of this unfortunate ducking was a violent cold, which for a time impaired the mental power which had directed the fluent tongue that had so often set the Trinitarian tables in a roar, and caused the fat sides of Dean B——— to shake by the half-hour together, and whose monstrous corporation, when once put in motion by the well-told tale, queer pun, pointed retort, or ludicrous accident, vibrated like a *pendulum*. The natural strength of D.'s constitution ultimately triumphed over the disease, save a severe deafness, which remained, a *memento* of the event, and defied the potency of medicine, though prescribed by the most favoured disciples of Æsculapius, or the votaries of *Quackiana*; and he was ever after obliged to use an *ear-trumpet*. One brilliant morning in June, he set out from Cambridge on a visit to his father, a sporting character, well-known at Tattersal's, and who lived within half an hour's ride of Bury St. Edmunds; but D———, meeting with an old acquaintance at Newmarket, he was persuaded to tarry awhile: accordingly, he put up his nag at the Ram, of that place, and adjourned with his friend to an elegant entertainment then about to grace the board. Having dissected the joints, fowls, &c. and demolished the pasties, the cloth was removed and the glass was filled to many a favourite toast; but D——— was, with reluctance, obliged to quit the converse of congenial souls and the delights of Bacchus, for H———, whither his destination led him, and for which place he again started at the fall of eve. Whether by the potency of the wine or some abstract philosophic speculation, no one can say; but certain it is, D——— was beguiled from the right course, and, after three hours' riding, he found his *pegasus* at a dead stand-still, where four cross-roads met, and in a part of the country to which he was an utter stranger. Misfortune seldom comes single-handed, and so it proved with poor D——; for the *direction-post*, which appeared full in his view, had been rendered useless by the attacks of time and little wanton boys; and as well might he have attempted to decipher the cabalistic characters of *Solomon's seal* as those on the post. Just at this nick of time he espied an old farmer in a jog-trot pace, making towards him, to his no small consolation; but so impatient was D——, that, before the farmer could approach him, he bawled out,—— " Hallo! my good man, can you tell me the way to my father's, Mr. D——, at H——, for I am quite at fault?"——" Lack-a-daisy, sir," answered Hodge, " you're mortally out o' your way; whoy, if it be that you want to go to your father's, you must go down *hin hinder** lane, and then turn round to the left over *yin yinder* common, then you'll see a *hol* and a *pightal*, and the old mills, and master's *noine* acre-piece o' *whate*; then keep along the right, and then the left, and down our home *medders*, and then up the"——" Stay, stay, my good friend! (exclaimed D——, in the midst of the farmer's harangue,) you don't know I am unfortunately *deaf*." At the same instant he began to pull out his faithful trumpet; but the farmer no sooner espied the shining end of it, than, setting spurs to his steed, he galloped off with the swiftness of the wind: for clod, not comprehending D——'s last words, mistook it for a blunderbuss, and D—— for a highwayman. Away went clod, and away went D—— after him, bawling out for the fellow to stop, and the fellow roaring out for mercy, not daring to look behind him.

* *Hin kinder, yin yinder,* common expressions in Suffolk, meaning, *a little further on.*

Thus they proceeded three or four miles, the *muzzle* of D——'s horse close upon the rump of the farmer's, till at last, coming to the Earl of Bristol's park, the farmer, espying a breach in the paling, rode through in a twink-ling, and got clear off, leaving poor D—— as he had found him. Fortunately, however, D—— discerned a cottage, which having gained, he was by the inmates put in the right way, with the consoling information that he had ten or twelve miles still to travel. He had the inex-pressible felicity of ending the adventure by making *dulce domum* about twelve at night.

" I TAKES 'EM AS THEY COME.

A Cantab, one day observing a *raggamuffin-looking* boy scratching his head at the door of Alderman Pur-chase, in Cambridge, where he was begging, and think-ing to pass a joke upon him, said, " So, Jack, you are picking them out, are you?"—" *Nah, sar*, retorted the urchin; " I *takes* 'em as they come!"

CATCHING COLD.

Dr. B——, well known in the University for his ur-banity of manners, is characterized for many eccentri-cities and singularities. He not unfrequently rises at four in the morning; and, that he may not disturb those who have no relish for so doing, lights his own fire. One morning, he sent express for his barber, a little dapper man of four feet some inches, to shave and dress him. When he entered, the doctor his usual custom, inquired how he was. Shaver, coughing, replied " he had caught a bad cold." " Have you so," said the doctor, smiling ; " how can it be otherwise, when you are *six* feet long, and your bed but *four*."

" PUPPIES NEVER SEE TILL THEY ARE NINE DAYS OLD."

It is related, that when the late Bishop of Bristol held the office of Vice-Chancellor of the University of Cambridge, he one day met a couple of undergraduates, who neglected to pay the accustomed compliment of *capping*, which has prevailed in the University from time immemorial. The bishop arrested their steps, and inquired the reason of the neglect. The two men, all trembling, begged his lordship's pardon, observing, they were *freshmen*, and did not know him. " How long have you been in Cambridge?" asked his lordship.—" Only *eight* days," was the reply. " Very good," said the bishop ; " *puppies* never see till they are *nine* days old !"

CHARACTERISTICS.

The late Dr. Brand was remarkable for his spirit of contradiction, and seemed to make it a part of his creed to differ with others. One extremely cold morning, in the month of January, returning from a walk, he was addressed by a friend with—" It is a very cold morning, doctor."—" I don't know that," was the doctor's observation, though he was at the instant covered with *snow*. At another time he happened to dine with some gentle-

men, and, after the cloth was removed, and general conversation introduced, the doctor, in a very dogmatical
manner, engrossed it almost entirely to himself, and in-
terlarded his observations with Greek and Latin quotations, to the annoyance of the company.   A gentleman
of no slight erudition, seated next the doctor, remarked to
him, " that he ought not to quote so much, as many of
the party did not understand it."—" And you are one of
them," observed the learned bear.

SMART RETORT.

Jemmy Gordon, a well-known character in Cambridge,
and an occasional visitor at the White Horse, Fetter
Lane, was one day walking down Trinity Street, a short
time after he had been employed at the *tread-mill* for a
month, with a view to remedy his abusive propensities
(which degradation did not sit on his mind with perfect
ease), when he was accosted by a collegian, from his
window, who knew Jemmy's antipathy to the event,
with, " How do you like the tread-mill, Jemmy ?"—" I
don't like your d—d ugly face !" was the reply.

A PEDANT CAUGHT NAPPING.

It may not be amiss to inform some of our readers, that
the only work which has come down to posterity from
the pen of Longinus (who held the important situation
of first minister to Zenobia, Queen of Palmyra, when it
was sacked by the Emperor Aurelian, by whom he was
shamefully put to death, although he had been pro-

nounced by his countrymen, the Greeks, the first critic and scholar of the age), is his (Περὶ Ὕψους), or *Treatise on the Sublime.*

A pedantic collegian was boasting, in a large party, of his extensive reading, adding, he had read Longinus over and over again, and thought him a dry fellow.—" Pray, sir," said a grave character near him, "have you ever read his Περὶ Ὕψους? (*Peri Hupsous.*)"—" No, sir," said the pedant; " unfortunately, I have read all his works except that."

SIMPLICITY OF MATHEMATICIANS.

The simplicity of mathematicians has often been commented on ; the following instance, a recent occurrence, is adduced, as exemplifying the truth of the observation, not as tending, by either its wit or brilliancy, to illuminate our pages. A gentleman, rather deeply read in the abstruse sciences, who stands high in his college examination, and whose head teems more with the calculation of integrals than with the trifles of general conversation, lately received a visit from the Rev. Mr. S———. The reverend gentleman found our mathematician poring over Locke on the Understanding, and had scarcely seated himself ere he was startled with, " Pray, sir, have you ever read Locke?"—"Yes, a little," was the reply.—" And do you think (continued the freshman), that Locke is correct where he says, *that the greatest capacity can contain the most ?*"—" Assuredly."—" Well, then, sir, I have been thinking to myself (added the freshman, measuring the extent of his own as he surveyed the head of the reverend visitor), that my head contains more brains than your's."

" MY FATHER WAS *PLUCKED* BEFORE ME."

When a man loses his degree from a want of capacity or negligence, he is said, in collegiate colloquiality, to be *plucked.* A Cantab, who had qualified himself by keeping his terms, &c. was about to enter the *Senate House,* for the purpose of being examined for his degree of B. A. when, struck with dismay at the formidable arrangement of desks, &c. which met his view, he turned his back upon the whole, declining to be examined, and exclaiming, at the time, " It will be no disgrace for me to lose my degree, for my father was *plucked* before me."

ELEGANT REPROOF.

Dr. Isaac Barrow remained faithful to the royal cause during the commonwealth; but, finding himself wholly neglected by the voluptuous and heedless Charles II., on his restoration, he reminded him of the services he had rendered him and the public, as a divine and loyalist, in the following distich:—

> " Te magis optabat rediturum, Carole, nemo ;
> Et nemo sensit te rediisse minus."

IN ENGLISH.

None more than I did restoration press ;
And none, than I, oh Charles ! have felt it less.

On the perusal of these lines, Charles was so struck with compunction, that he ordered the first vacant ecclesiastical dignity to be conferred on Barrow; this was accordingly done, but it came too late in the day for Barrow to enjoy it. So true is the observation often made, "that the Stuarts never rewarded their friends or punished their foes."

SOMNAMBULISM.

A fellow of a certain college in Cambridge one day fell asleep during the performance of divine service, and his busy imagination conveyed him to his own rooms. Occupied with an idea that his coal-dealer, who was chapel clerk, had overcharged him, he bawled out, "John N——, I wish you'd let me have my coals at the same price as other people have them!"

REX HUJUS LOCI.

Dr. ——, then head of a certain college in Cambridge, understanding from his spouse, who was a thrifty matron, and a crown unto a husband, that their Yorkshire servant, John, used too much candle in the stable, he sent for him, and inquired what he meant by it?—— "Please, zur," said John, "You knaw as how oi uses things as niggardlike as pozzible. Howbeet, zur, won maun have a bit o' rushlight at noight, to see whon's way about the proimizes. "True, true, John," said the doctor, who was remarkable for his urbanity; "true, but you overdo the thing." "How so, zur?" said John. "How so, fellow!" exclaimed the doctor, "How so! what d'ye mean by how-soing me over? You're insolent, fellow, very insolent. You use too much candle a great deal, and are insolent into the bargain; don't you know, fellow, I'm *king of this place?*—" If so be, zur," said John, " as how you be *koing* o' this place, perhaps your majesty will give me moy discharge?" It is needless to add Yorky was dismissed the service; and, when the circumstances came to be known, the learned doctor retained his regal appellation for many years.

THE RETORT CUTTING.

Bishops Sherlock and Hoadly were both freshmen of the same year, at Catherine Hall, Cambridge. The classical subject in which they were first lectured, was Tully's Offices, and it so happened, one morning, that Hoadly received a compliment from the tutor for the excellence of his construing. Sherlock, a little vexed at the preference shown to his rival (for such they then were), and, thinking to bore Hoadly by the remark, said, when they left the lecture-room, " Ben, you made good use of L'Estrange's *translation* to-day."—" Why, no, Tom," retorted Hoadly, " I did not, for I had not got one; and I forgot to borrow *your's*, which, I am told, is the only one in the college."

A MARVELLOUS HINT.

At a party of which the late Dr. Brand happened to make one, many stories were related by one of the gentlemen, for the entertainment of the company, of a most *marvellous* description. A pause occurring in the conversation, the doctor commenced by saying,—" Gentlemen, I will tell my tale. In a country village," continued the doctor, "lived a butcher, who had the curiosity, one day, to view the adjacent country from the top of the village steeple, and, for that purpose, he was shown up by the clerk of the parish. Soon after they had reached the top, the bells began to ring, which caused the steeple to rock from one side to the other with such velocity, that the butcher, unable to bear the effect (which completely addled his brains), leaped from the top; but reflecting, on his way down, of the eminent risk he ran in alighting, he suddenly drew his knife from its sheath, stuck it in the wall, and there hung dangling by it, like a hat on a peg, till some persons, having obtained a ladder, lifted him down."——"That must be a lie!" exclaimed the person who had before amused the company so much.—— "And, pray, what have you been telling the whole evening?" said the doctor. Our gentleman was *mum*.

COUPLET FOR COUPLET.

Dr. John Jegon, formerly Master of Benet, or Corpus Christi College, Cambridge, for some serious offence, *fined* all the undergraduates of his own college; and, instead of applying the money to any private use, as was the custom, he ordered that the college hall should be whitewashed with it: whereupon one of the students, a wag in his way, hung on the skreen the following couplet:—

" Doctor John Jegon, of Benét College master,
  Brake the scholars' heads, and gave the wall a plaster."

The doctor, passing through the hall next day, saw the

above, and, not being wanting in wit, subscribed, *extempore*,—

" Knew I but the wag that writ these verses in bravery,
　I'd commend him for his wit, but whip him for his
　　knavery."

SARCASTIC EPIGRAM.

When death unrelentingly cut short the career of Porson, and the election of a Greek professor took place, a Cantab (who was cotemporary with him at a public school) wrote the following epigram on one of the candidates :—

EPIGRAM.

Actum est Porsono ! descendit " Φοιβος Αχαιων :"
M**kius en ! lampas nil, nisi nigra manet.

TRANSLATED.

Lo ! Porson's dead ! the sun of Greece is sunk,
And nought is left but farthing-rushlight, M**k.

ALL WAITERS.

In St. John's Hall, one day, during dinner, there happened to be a great paucity of *waiters*. A gentleman, impatient at the delay, at length exclaimed, " D——n it, we can't get a *waiter !*"—" The devil we can't," said Mr. K——, who sat opposite, " I think we are *all waiters*."

A BLUNDER.

A reverend gentleman of Queen's College, whose duty it was, being unable to perform divine service at his church, in Chesterton, near Cambridge, deputed a divine of Trinity College, for the Sunday. The Trinitarian, who dined at a lady's in the parish, before service, unwittingly left his sermon on the table. Having finished the prayers, and mounted the pulpit, he put his hand in his coat-pocket for his sermon; but, alas! it was not there. However, with great presence of mind, he leaned over the desk and whispered to the clerk (who happened unfortunately to be deaf, and, withal, like most village clerks, a rustic),—" Run, fetch my sermon, which I left on the table in Mrs. Chitteau's parlour."—Amen, misunderstanding the words, immediately bawled out, with stentorian voice, " This is to give notice, that the sermon will be preached, this afternoon, in Mrs. Chitteau's parlour."

A MUSICAL BLOW-UP.

The Rev. Mr. B——, when residing at Canterbury, was reckoned a good violencello-player; but he was not more distinguished for his expression on the instrument, than for the peculiar appearance of feature whilst playing it. In fact, when lost in the midst of the adagios of Corelli or Avison, the muscles of his face all sympathized with his fiddle-stick, and kept up a reciprocal movement. His sight, being dim, obliged him very often to snuff the candles, and, when he came to a bar's rest, in lieu of snuffers, he generally employed his fingers in

I

hat office; and, lest he should offend the good house-
wife by this dirty trick of his, he used to thrust the *spoils*
into the *sound-holes* of his violencello. A waggish friend
of his, who had observed B——'s whim, resolved to enjoy himself " at the parson's expense," as he termed it;
and, for that purpose, he popped a quantity of gun-pow-
der into B——'s instrument. The rest were informed of
the trick, and of course kept at a respectable distance.
The tea equipage being removed, music became the order of
the evening, and, after B—— had tuned his instrument,
and drawn his stand near enough to snuff his candles with
ease, feeling himself in the meridian of his glory, he
lashed away at Vanhall's 47th. B—— came to a bar's
rest, the candles were snuffed, and he thrust the ignited
wick into the usual place;—*fit fragor,* and bang went the
fiddle to pieces.

AN ILLUSTRATION.

Milton, the British Homer, and prince of modern
poets, in his latter days, and when he was blind (a thing
some men do with their eyes open), married a *shrew*.
The Duke of Buckingham, one day, in Milton's hearing,
called her a *rose.* " I am no judge of flowers," observed Milton, " but it may be so, for I feel the *thorns*
daily."

NON PAR ERIS.

When the mastership of Harrow School became vacant, Dr. Parr applied for it, but was opposed by a learned gentleman, who was detested by the boys on account
of his temper. At a meeting, previous to the election of
a master, the latter gentleman was endeavouring to per-

suade the boys, in a long harangue, that no person was so
well qualified for the mastership as himself. At last
however, breathless with speechifying, he made a momentary pause, when one of his juvenile auditors, with
most witty and pretty classical allusion, vociferated,—

" Si te ruperis, non *par* eris."

(If you burst yourself, you'll never equal Parr). A fine
compliment to the doctor, alluding to Horace's Fable of
the Frog and the Ox. The pun on the word *par* was so
rapturously received, that the doctor's opponent was
obliged to sit down amidst the laughter of the whole
assembly.

A NEW READING.

At a party of Cantabs, soon after the late queen's
trial, one of the gentlemen proposed as a toast, " *the
queen's pure innocence.*" Upon which another of the
party rose and said, " I have no objection to the toast
with the substitution of a letter." To which innovation
the proposer consenting, he gave, " the queen's pure *in
no sense.*"

DOUBLE ENTENDRE.

A person ycleped *Danger* kept a public inn on the
road from Cambridge to Huntingdon. Another inn
nearly opposite his own, happening to become vacant
Danger applied for it, thinking it a more eligible situation; in fact, Danger changed sides. Danger's late residence was, in consequence, in want of a master, and

dvertised to be let.   A tenant was soon found, who,
eing a waggish fellow, and, withal, desirous that the
aange of proprietors should be known to wayfaring
nen, posted over his door, on a board, " *No Danger
re now.*"   Mr. Danger was sorely troubled at these
ords, conceiving that they intended to imply something
ore than a mere change of masters, and took an oppor-
inity of mentioning the circumstance to some Cantabs,
ho called at his house soon after ; one of them advised
im to place over his door, in equally conspicuous cha-
ucters, " *Danger from the other side of the way.*"   This
nuble entendre was highly relished, and many, in conse-
ience, were often induced to seek *Danger*.

" A RARE MATHEMATICAL WIND."

The late Professor Vince, one morning (several trees
ving been blown down the night previous), meeting a
iend in the walks of St. John's College, Cambridge,
as accosted with, " How d'ye do, sir ? quite a bluster-
g wind this."—" Yes," answered Vince, " it's a rare
athematical wind."—" Mathematical wind !" exclaimed
e other, " How so ?"—" Why," replied Vince, " it has
tracted a great many *roots* !"

MILTON'S BEAUTY.

The beauty of Milton, during the period that he pur-
ed his studies at the University of Cambridge, and to a
uch more subsequent period, was a subject upon which
friends frequently dwelt.   Wandering one day during

the summer, as was his custom, beyond the precincts of
the university, he at length became heated and fatigued,
and, seeking the shade of a spreading tree, he laid himself down to meditate, and soon fell asleep.   During the
time that he slumbered, two foreign ladies passed near
the spot in a carriage, who, astonished at the loveliness
of his appearance, in the heat of their admiration
alighted, and viewing him, as they thought, unperceived,
the youngest, who was extremely handsome, drew a
pencil from her pocket, and having written some lines
upon a piece of paper, put it with a trembling hand into
Milton's.   They then entered their carriage and proceeded on their journey.   Some of his academic friends
had silently observed this adventure, undiscovered by the
fair admirers, not knowing it was their friend Milton
who was unconsciously playing the enchanter: but, approaching the spot, they recognised him, and, awaking
him, told him what had passed.   Milton opened the
paper, and, to his no small surprise, read the following
verses from the Italian poet, Guarini :—

> " Oechi, stelle mortali,
> Ministri de mici mali,
> Se chiusi m'accidete,
> Apperti che farere?"

TRANSLATED.

> O eyes! O mortal stars! I find ye
> Authors of lovely pangs that blind me :
> If thus when shut you've power to wound me,
> Open, alas! how hadst thou bound me?

Milton was eager to discover the fair *incognita*, and i

was probably this incident which afterwards carried him to Italy, in hopes of discovering her abode, but in vain. The idea that Milton had formed of his unknown admirer so fanned his poetic fervour, that his own times, the present, and the latest posterity, must probably feel indebted to it for several of the most beautiful and impassioned passages in his *Paradise Lost;* and from the above incident, perhaps, he caught the idea of that inimitable poem.

FICTION AND TRUTH.

Waller, the poet, who was bred at King's College, Cambridge, wrote a fine panegyric on Cromwell, when he assumed the protectorship. Upon the restoration of Charles, Waller wrote another in praise of him, and presented it to the king in person. After his majesty had read the poem, he told Waller that he wrote a better on Cromwell. " Please your majesty," said Waller, like a true courtier, " we poets are always more happy in *fiction* than in *truth.*"

"SLEEP ON, AND TAKE YOUR REST."

A wit at Cambridge, in the days of King James, was appointed to preach at St. Marie's, before the Vice-chancellor and the heads of the universitie, who formerlie had observed the drowsiness of the Vice-chancellor, and thereupon took this place of Scripture for his text, ' *What! cannot ye watch one hour!*" At everie division, he concluded with his text, which, by reason of the Vice-chancellor sitting so near the pulpit, often awaked him.

This was so noted by the wits of those daies, that it was the talk of the whole universitie, and, withal, it did so nettle the Vice-chancellor, that he complained to the Archbishop of Canterburie, who, willing to redress him, sent for this scholar up to London, to defend himself against this crime laid to his charge by the Vice-chancellor; where coming, he gave so many proofs of his extraordinary wit, that the archbishop enjoined him to preach before King James; to which, after some excuses, he at length consented, and, coming into the pulpit, begins,—*James the First and the Sixth, waver not,*—meaning the first king of England and the sixth of Scotland. At first, the king was somewhat amazed at the text, but, in the end, he was so well pleased with the sermon, that he made the preacher one of his chaplains in ordinary. After this advancement, the archbishop sent him down to Cambridge to make his recantation to the Vice-chancellor, and to take leave of the university, which he accordingly did, in a sermon, for which he took the latter part of the verse of his former text, *Sleep on now, and take your rest.* Concluding his sermon, he made his apology to the vice-chancellor, saying, " Whereas, I said before," which gave offence, " *what, cannot ye watch one hour?* I say now, *sleep on, and take your rest,*" and so left the universitie.

" APROPOS."

The Rev. George Harvest, who had been his schoolfellow at Eton, came down to Cambridge to vote for Lord Sandwich, when he stood candidate for the chancellorship of that university. At a dinner given to his

riends on the occasion, his lordship, joking him on some
of their school-boy tricks, in the simplicity of his heart,
Harvest suddenly exclaimed, "*Apropos!* where do you
derive your name of *Jemmy Twitcher?*"—"Why,"
answered his lordship, "from some foolish fellow or
other."—"No, no," interrupted Harvest, "it is not
some, but every body calls you so." His lordship being
seated near the pudding, for which he knew Harvest had
no slight relish, put a large slice on his plate, which
Harvest immediately attacked, which had the desired effect of putting an end to his *apropos.*

"ALAS! WE CAN'T."

At a party where there was no lack of either good
port, good fellowship, or harmony, one of the gentlemen proposed, at the end of a song, they should take a
glass. "Would we could have a *lass!*" exclaimed a second. "*A—las!* we can't," was the *bewail-instanter* of
a third.

SIR BUSICK HARWOOD AND THE CANDLE AND LANTERN.

During the period Sir Busick Harwood was professor of
anatomy in the University of Cambridge, he was called
in, in a case of some difficulty, by the friends of a patient, who were anxious for his opinion of the malady.
Not approving the treatment which had been pursued towards the invalid, and, in answer to his inquiry, being
told the name of the medical man who had previously

prescribed, Sir Busick exclaimed, perhaps with more truth than feeling,—"He! if he were to descend into the patient's stomach with a *candle and lantern*, when he ascended he would not be able to name the complaint."

HOCK *versus* FALERNIAN.

As some Peter-house fellows, one day, as I have heard,
Were disputing which liquor old *Horace* preferred,
While some were for this sort, and others for that,
And backed their belief with quotations quite pat;
Whilst, in spite of their joking, the contest ran high,
And some would have quarrell'd, but couldn't tell why:
Old P——ne, who, till now, had not moved tongue or
    breech,
Put an end to the war by this comical speech:——
" You may talk of your wines, with a name purely
    classic,
Such as Chiar, Falernian, Lesbian, and Massic;
But of this I am sure, and it worthy of note is,
Hock, hock was his liquor,—' *Hoc erat in votis!* '"*

A LONG-WINDED SERMON.

The erudite Dr. Isaac Barrow, who, it is well known, was tutor to Sir Isaac Newton, during his residence as an undergraduate at Trinity College, Cambridge, was complimented, by King Charles II., with the title of the best scholar of the age, but called him an unfair one; "for," said the king, " when he once begins a subject, he says so much on it, that nobody can say anything on the

* Vide Hor. Sat. 6. lib. 2.

same point after him." Barrow was certainly very long-winded, and could discern as well as, or better than, any of his cotemporaries, all the positions in which a thesis could be taken; and, as he reasoned on them in a regular syllogistic style, he seldom omitted anything, pertinent to the proof, for others to say after him. Dr. Pope, in his life of Seth Ward, Bishop of Salisbury, relates the following curious anecdote of him :—Barrow, being appointed to preach in Westminster Abbey, divided his discourse into two parts. The first, on *lies;* and the second, on *slander.* He was *four* hours delivering the *first part*, so fully had he entered into the subject. The congregation sneaked off, but the dean and prebends could not, with propriety, leave till the conclusion of the sermon. But, at last, thinking it would be like Aristotle's world, ατελυταιον (without limit), they sent a chorister to desire the organist to draw out his trumpet and open-diapason stop, and play the doctor down. This was instantly done. Dr. Pope afterwards asked Barrow " if he did not feel himself distressed in the lungs after such a spell at preaching ?"—" Not at all," was his reply, " I was only a little tired with standing."

SETTLING A POINT OF PRECEDENCE.

On a time, a question arose in the University of Cambridge, between the doctors of law and the doctors of medicine, as to which ought to take precedence of the other on public occasions. It was referred to the Chancellor, who facetiously inquired whether the *thief* or the *hangman* preceded at an execution, and, being told that the thief usually took the lead on such occasions,—" Well, then," he replied, " let the doctors in law have the precedence, and the doctors of medicine be next in rank." This humorous observation set the point in dispute at rest.

" JOVIAL DAYS."

A party of Johnians were one day assembled in order to moisten the inward man with a bumper of wine, when the conversation turned upon a discussion of the different festivals and days—amongst others, sidereal and solar days were named. A dry fish, who looked anything but a punster, putting a bumper to his lips, observed, " I think we should have *jovial days* as well."

THE MITRE.

One of the wooden *mitres* carved by Grin. Gibbon over a prebend's stall in the cathedral church of Canterbury happening to become loose, Jessy White, the surveyor of that edifice, inquired of the dean whether he should make it fast—" for, perhaps," said Jessy, " it may fall on your reverence's head." " Well! Jessy, suppose it does," answered the humorous Cantab,— " suppose it does fall on my head, I don't know that a mitre falling on my head would hurt it."

A COMPLIMENT RETURNED IN FULL.

Porson once happened to be in the company of Dr. Jackson, an Oxonian, who, thinking to pay the learned professor a flattering compliment, said to him, " Porson,

ou are the only man that ever left the University of
Cambridge, learned in Greek." The professor, whose
wit, like the " *whoop halloo!*" of a keen sportsman when
his dogs are at fault, was always at command, responded
to the doctor's flattery, " And you, doctor, are the only
man that ever left Oxford with any learning at all."

HYDROSTATICAL EXPERIMENT.

Dr. Craven, late Master of St. John's College, excited
the wrath of a waggish student, by indulging him with
an *imposition*, for some irregularity of conduct. *Sky par-
our* claimed the honour of being inhabited by this aspir-
ant to philosophical fame, when, watching an opportunity, as the venerable master was sunning himself beside
the college walls, he proceeded to discharge the contents
of a huge stone jar upon his devoted head : unfortunately, the jar followed the water, and was near inflict-
ing on the learned doctor the fate of Æschines. Enraged at this, Dr. Craven issued a summons, com-
manding the immediate attendance of the inhabitant of
that room from whence the pitcher had fallen. Upon
his entrance, the doctor exclaimed, " Young man—young
man, you had nearly killed your poor old master—you
had nearly killed me;" when the unabashed culprit, with
the most perfect *nonchulance*, replied, " I was merely
trying some *hydrostatical* experiments." " Hydrostatical
experiments!" exclaimed the enraged master, thrown
entirely off his guard by the cool answer of the Johnian,
" I'd thank you, young man, when next you pursue your
hydrostatical labours, not to use such a d——d large
pitcher."

NOVEL RECEPTION OF A CREDITOR.

A gentleman of St. John's College was very fond of pursuing electrical and other experiments; indeed, so much was he attached to it, that it might justly be denominated his *hobby;* and he would occasionally expend money in the purchase of *apparatus,* which ought, in justice, to have liquidated debts previously contracted:— so Mr. Bishop, the tailor, thought; and who, accordingly, with a view of *dunning* the Cantab, after he had mounted the stone staircase which led to the " parlour next to the sky," and in vain beat a *tattoo* upon the *double* doors, would slowly descend again. This had been repeated so often to the annoyance of the Johnian, that he resolved at once to cure poor Snip of his peregrinating propensities: To this end, he charged his electrical machine more than ordinarily, and fixed the conductor to the latch of the door. Bishop, watched by the Johnian, as usual, ascended the staircase at the expected hour, and was not a little overjoyed to behold but one door between him and *client.* He gave a gentle rat-tat: " Come in," echoed from the interior;—he joyfully grasped the brass nob :—the *electric* shock was communicated to his sensitive, but not very robust frame, with so much force, that, more dead than alive, he made a precipitate retreat—nor was he in haste to renew his visit.

CRITICS.

Besides great integrity, great humanity, and other qualities alike honourable, Dr. Jortin was of a pleasant and facetious turn. He had a great respect and fondness for critical learning, which he much cultivated, and thought the restoration of letters and the civilization of Europe to depend on it. He could not bear to see it contemptuously treated, and did not spare those who had done so. He thus speaks of an oration of Julius Cæsar Scaliger, whom he esteemed one of those insolent critics:—" The whole is seasoned with arrogance, vanity, self-applause, spite, and scurrility, the usual ornaments, not of a meek and quiet spirit, but of a ruffian and a bruiser in the republic of letters."

CURIOUS ADVERTISEMENT.

The following advertisement, drawn up by an alderman of the town of Cambridge, some years ago, is here inserted, as a specimen of singular felicity of expression:—

" Whereas a multiplicity of damages are frequently occurred by damages of outrageous accidents of fire, we, whose names are underwritten, have thought proper, that the necessity of an engine ought, by us, for the better preventing of which, by the accidents of Almighty God, may happen, to make a rate to gather benevolence for better propagating such instruments."

RABBITS UNDERSTANDING LATIN.

Some young Cantabs, going a-hunting, enjoined one of the company, who was usually very talkative, to preserve silence, or he would frighten away the game. However, on espying a number of rabbits, he vociferously exclaimed, " *Ecce! multi cunniculi!*" when they disappeared in a moment. Being chid by his companions, he replied, "Who would have thought the rabbits understood Latin?"

THE GREAT CALF.

A company disputing on the superiority of Oxford to Cambridge, a gentleman present remarked that the decision could not affect him, because he was educated at both:—"That," said an old gentleman present, "puts me in mind of a calf, which I remember, when I was a lad, was suckled by two cows." "Really," said the university gentleman; "and pray, sir, what was the consequence?" "Why, sir, he turned out the *greatest calf I ever saw in my life.*"

A DELICATE COMPLIMENT.

Dr. Parr, who, it is well known, is not very partial to the "*thea linensis*," although lauded so warmly by a French writer as "*nostris gratissima musis*," being invited to take *tea* by a lady, with true classic wit and refined gallantry, uttered the following delicate compliment :— "Non possum *tea* cum vivere, nec sine *te!*"

A MATHEMATICIAN'S EPITHALAMIUM,

BY A GENTLEMAN OF TRINITY COLLEGE, CAMBRIDGE.

Though the *sum*, my dear wife, of the days of thy life
 Should be greater, at length, than *infinity*,—
Though wrinkles should trace their deep *curves* on thy
 face,
 I would love thee, for years, *sine limite.*

hile the years roll away and our bodies decay,
Our love shall know no *aberrations* ;
t firmly conjoined we will always be found,
Like *impossible roots in equations*.

alous fears too, I ween, shall ne'er intervene,
Perturbing our peaceful community ;
r *divisions* shall never love's *vinculum* sever,
Nor *eliminate concord and unity*.

sweet conversations and chaste oscillations
Our souls we will daily *expand* ;
gravity, too, we will bid long adieu,
And all fear of *depression* withstand.

thy wishes I ne'er will *incline* a *surd* ear,—
My direction thou ever shalt be ;
nd each thought of thy mind, when imparted, shall find
A sure *co-efficient* in me.

nd *functions* so *prime*, in the process of time,
Shall sweet little *increments generate*,
Vho shall grow up as fair as the parents now are,
Or *approximate* to them, at any rate.

hus I, love, and you, *combined, two and two*,
Shall proceed in *harmonic progression*—
n *reciprocal* pleasure, which admits of no *measure*—
For which language supplies no *expression*.

ind think not, my Mary, my affections will *vary*—
That my love will be quickly *'vanescent* ;
'or round thee my soul in its *orbit* shall roll,
Till my body in earth lie *quiescent*.

SPOILING A COMPLIMENT.

During the time that Paley was staying with the Bishop of Durham, an old clergyman perchance visited the palace, who asserted, during conversation, " Although he had been married almost forty years, he had never had the slightest difference with his wife." The bishop, much pleased with so rare an instance of connubial felicity, was on the very point of complimenting the divine, when Paley archly observed, " Don't you think, my lord, it must have been very flat ?"

OH, ASS !

Porson was one day conversing in Latin with a certain learned Theban, from the sister university, when the latter, wishing to convince the professor that he was better acquainted with the writings of Cicero than any man living, affirmed that he had spent *thirteen years* " *in perlegendo Cicerone ;*" to which the Greek professor, with admirable wit, replied, " *And echo answered, ovε.*" (Oh, ass !)

CURE FOR A DISEASE.

A Cantab, who happened to be under Sir Busick Harwood, when professor, was enjoined to live temperately, as a cure for his malady. The doctor called upon him one day, and found him enjoying himself over a bottle of Madeira. " Ah, doctor !" exclaimed the patient, at the same time reaching out his hand to bid him welcome, " I am glad to see you ; you are just in time to

taste the first bottle of some prime Madeira!"   "Ah!"
replied Sir Busick, "these bottles of Madeira will never
do—they are the cause of all your sufferings!"   "Are
they so?" cried the patient, "then fill your glass, my
dear doctor; for, since we know the cause, the sooner
we get rid of it the better."

JEMMY GORDON.

Jemmy Gordon, *nimis notus omnibus, ignotus sibi*, the
well-known writer of many a *theme* and *declamation* for
varmint-men, alias *non-reading* Cantabs, who may be said
to merit the cognomen of *Trismegistus*, having been complimented by an acquaintance on the result of one of his
themes, to which the prize of a certain college was award-
ed, quaintly enough replied, " It is no great credit to be
first in an *ass-race*."

THE EXCEPTION.

When England was threatened with invasion by
France, a certain corporation agreed to form a volunteer
corps, on condition that they should not be obliged to
quit the country. Their proposal was submitted to Mr.
Pitt, the premier, who facetiously observed, he had no
objection to the terms, if they would permit him to add,
" *except* in case of invasion."

FIE! ROWE!

The Cocoa-Tree Tavern, in St. James's Street, in those
days designated the *Wits' Coffee-House*, was the frequent
resort of the celebrated Cantab, Dr. Garth. He was one

morning seated there, conversing with some persons of rank, when Rowe, the poet, well known as a dramatic writer and commentator on Shakspeare, entered, and seated himself in an opposite box to that in which was the doctor and his friends. Rowe was not only inattentive to his dress and appearance, but insufferably vain, and fond of being noticed by persons of consequence. He endeavoured for some time to catch the doctor's eye, but, failing, he desired the waiter to ask for his snuff-box, which he knew to be a valuable one, set with diamonds, which had been presented to Garth by some foreign prince. After taking a pinch, he returned it; but asked for it so repeatedly, that Garth, out of all patience, and perceiving his drift, wrote on the lid the two Greek characters—Φ. P. (Phi Rho). This the mortified poet interpreted FIE! ROWE! and instantly quitted the room.

To this specimen of the doctor's wit may be added the following example of his humanity and compassion. The doctor was one day detained in his chariot, in a narrow street, near Covent Garden, through a crowd collected to witness a bruising-match between two Amazonian ladies of the Billingsgate tribe, when an old woman hobbled up to him, and begged him "for God's sake to *take a look* at her husband, who was in a *mortal bad way*;" adding, "I know you are a sweet-tempered gentleman, as well as a *cute* doctor, so make bold to ar your advice." The doctor, not a jot offended at her liberty of speech, immediately quitted his chariot, and followed her to her abode of misery, where he found that the patient wanted *food* rather than physic; and, finding from their answers to his questions, that they deserved

compassion, taking out his pencil, he wrote the following infallible *prescription* for such cases, addressed to his
banker—" Pay the bearer £10."

NOVEL PAYMENT OF A DEBT.

That celebrated Cantab—" *O rare Ben Jonson,*" was
one day invited to dine with a vintner, in whose books
his name had appeared on the debtor's side for no in-
considerable period, without any equivalent being likely
to appear under the term creditor.   The wine, a beverage of which our poet was not a little fond, had gone
merrily round, when the vintner declared he would forgive Ben his debt, if he could immediately answer him
the following questions :—" What God is best pleased
with ?—What the devil is best pleased with ?—What the
world is best pleased with ?—And what he was best
pleased with ?"   Ben, under the inspiration of the jolly
god, gave an immediate answer in the following admirable impromptu :—

" God is best pleased when men forsake their sin ;
    The devil's best pleased when they persist therein ;
    The world's best pleased when thou dost sell good wine ;
    And you're best pleased when I do pay for mine."

A FOOL CONFIRMED.

That Dr. Parr is neither very choice nor delicate in his
epithets, when his *temper*-ature is raised above summer
heat, is no secret to those who may have fallen under

his lash. He once called a clergyman a *fool*, and the
was probably some truth in his application of the wor
The clergyman, however, being of a different opinio
declared he would complain to the bishop of the usag
"Do so," added the learned Grecian, "and my Lo
Bishop will *confirm* you."

PORSON OR THE DEVIL.

Porson was once travelling in a stage-coach, when
young Oxonian, fresh from college, was amusing th
ladies with a variety of small talk, to which he added
quotation, as he said, from Sophocles. A Greek qu
tation, and in a stage-coach too, roused our professo
who, in a dog-sleep, was slumbering in one corner o
the vehicle. Rubbing his eyes, "I think, young gen
tleman," said Porson, "you just now favoured us with
quotation from Sophocles; I don't happen to recolle
it there." "Oh? Sir," replied the Oxonian, "the quo
tation is word for word as I repeated it, and in Sopho
cles too; but I suspect, Sir, it is some time since yo
were at college." Porson, applying his hand to hi
great coat, took out a small pocket edition of Sophocles
and handed it to our tyro, saying he should be much
obliged if he would show him the passage in that littl
book. Having rummaged the pages for some time,
"Upon second thoughts," said the Oxonian, "I now
recollect 'tis in Euripides."—"Then," said the professor,
putting his hand into his pocket, and handing him a si
milar edition of that author," perhaps you will be so
good as to find it for me in that little book."—He re-

urned again to his task, but with no better success, mut-
ering to himself—"Curse me if ever I quote Greek
again in a coach." The ladies tittered: at last, "Bless
me, Sir," said he, "how dull I am! I recollect now,—
yes, yes, I perfectly remember, the passage is in Æschy-
us." This inexorable professor applied again to his in-
xhaustable pocket, and was in the act of handing an
Æschylus to the astonished freshman, when he vocife-
ated—"Stop the coach,—hollo,—coachman let me out, I
ay,—instantly let me out; there's a fellow here has got
he whole Bodleian Library in his pocket; let me out,
: say—let me out, he must be Porson or the Devil;"

Of this distinguished character, the following is a
lassical anecdote, related of the early proof he gave of
us acute and extraordinary talents. When at a public
chool, the following subject for a theme was handed
o him by the master :—

"*Cæsare occiso, an Brutus benefecit, aut malefecit.*"

A game being proposed, he joined the sports among
he rest of the scholars, and the theme was forgot. When
alled upon for his performance, he was astonished, on
eference to his writing-folio, to find it quite unpre-
ared ; the call, however, was imperative, and the mo-
nents but few and precious,—indeed, so few as to pre-
lude the possibility of a laboured article ; and, snatching
up a pen, he scrawled the following, which he handed
o the master, and which was received with no small
urprise, though with infinite satisfaction :—

"Nec *bene*-fecit, nec *male*-fecit, sed interfecit."

C. versus K.

A country gentleman, who had turned his attention to letters, wrote to a learned Johnian, now resident in Cambridge, desiring his opinion, as to whether C, in the word *stoicism*, ought not to be pronounced like K. To which the Cantab returned the following laconic answer :——

" Had *Kikero* (Cicero) been an Englishman, I do not think we should have met with *Stoikism*, *Kritikism*, *Astrikism*, or any other kism in his writings."

PRAISE OF CAMBRIDGE ALE.

Cambridge ale, particularly " Audit," has been long celebrated for its inspiring qualities. A certain Trinitarian, who, though no *barker*, is well known among the literati for his *classical acumen*, on receiving a present of *Audit*, exclaimed :——

" *All hail* to the *ale!* It sheds a *halo* round my *head*."

ARCHBISHOP MOUNTAIN.

This reverend prelate raised himself, by his remarkably facetious turn, from being the son of a humble individual, to the valuable see of Durham. In the reign of George the Second, the see of York becoming vacant, the king, being at a loss for a fit person to fill so exalted a situation, asked the opinion of the doctor, who

vittily replied to the query of his majesty, by the
ollowing appropriate quotation from Scripture.—"Hadst
hou faith as a grain of mustard-seed, thou wouldst say
o this *Mountain*," laying his hand on his breast as he
poke, " be removed, and be cast into the sea (*see*)." The
.ing laughed heartily at the conceit, and conferred the
refernient on the doctor.

ALLITERATION.

Among the best specimens of alliteration, may be
anked the well-known lines on the celebrated Cardinal
Volsey :—

" Begot by butchers, but by bishops bred,
How high his honour holds his haughty head !"

But the following unpublished sally, by the erudite
Dr. Parr, is not a whit inferior.—In a company con-
isting principally of divines, the conversation naturally
urned on the merits of the late head of the church, who
vas thus characterized by the learned and eccentric
loctor, in reply to one of the gentlemen :—" Sir, he is
poor paltry prelate, proud of petty popularity, and
erpetually preaching to petticoats."

PORSON versus DR. JOWETT.

Dr. Jowett, who was a *small* man, and had an itching
or the *rus in urbe*, was permitted by the head of his
ollege to cultivate a strip of vacant ground. This gave

rise to some *jeux d'esprit* among the wags of the university, which induced him to alter it into a plot of gravel
This being shown to Porson, he burst forth with the following

EXTEMPORANEOUS LINES.

A *little* garden *little* Jowett made,
    And fenced it with a *little* pallisade ;
Because this garden made a little talk,
    He changed it to a *little* gravel walk ;
And now, if more you'd know of *little* Jowett,
A *little* time, it will a *little* show it.

PARODY ON GRAY's BARD.

BY THE LATE MARMADUKE LAWSON, ESQ. M. P.

*Occasioned by the Suppression of the Society, in Cam-
bridge, by the Vice-Chancellor, A. D. 1817, called*

THE UNION.

I. 1.

" Ruin seize thee, senseless prig !
    Confusion on thy ' optics ' wait ;
Though praised by many a Johnian pig,
    They crowd the shop in fruitless state.

" Hood nor doctor's scarlet gown,
Nor N—th nor P—th, shall win renown ;
Nor save thy secret soul from nightly fears,
The UNION's curse, the UNION's tears."

Such were the sounds that o'er the pedant pride
    Of W—d, the Johnian, scattered wild dismay,

As down the flags of Petty-Cury's* side
   He would with toilsome march his long array;
Stout T——th——m stood aghast with puffy face——
"To arms," cried Beverly,† and shook his quiv'ring
   mace.

I. 2.

At a window, which on high
   Frowns o'er the market-place below,
With trousers‡ on, and haggard eye,
   A member stood immersed in woe.
His tattered gown and greasy hair
Streamed like a dishclout to the onion'd air,
And, with a voice that well might beat the crier,
Struck the deep sorrows of his lyre.——

Hark! how each butcher's stall, and mightier shop,
Sighs to the market's clattering row beneath;

* The name of the street in which the UNION was held.
† One of the Esquire Bedells, who bear the mace before
the Vice-chancellor.
‡ The savage despair of the member is finely portrayed
by the trousers, as a total indifference to moral guilt or
personal danger is argued by his thus appearing before the
Vice-chancellor; that gentleman *justly* regards the wearing of them as the most atrocious of moral offences, and
having *deservedly* excluded a distinguished wrangler, who
had been guilty of wearing them, from a fellowship of his
college :——

   "Crure tenus medio tunicas succingere debet."
                      Juv. Sat. 6.

'or thee the women's squall, the cleaver's chop,
 Revenge on thee in hoarser murmurs breathe.
✓ocal no more, since Monday's fatal night,
 To Thirlwall's* keen remark, or Sheridan's* wild flight.

I. 3.

Mute now is Raymond's* tongue,
 That hushed the club to sleep;
The patriot Whitcomb* now has ceased to rail :
 Waiters, in vain ye weep.
Lawson, whose annual song
 Made the RED LION† wag his raptur'd tail.
Dear lost companions in the spouting art,
 Dear as the common smoking in the hall,
Dear as the *Audit Ale*, that warms my heart,
 Ye fell amidst the dying UNION's fall.

II. 1.

Weave the warp, and weave the woof,
 The winding sheet of J——mmy's race;
Give ample room and verge enough—
 To mark revenge, defeat, disgrace.
Mark the month, and mark the day,
The senate echoing widely with the fray;
Commoner, sizar, pensioner, and snob,
Shouts of an undergraduate mob.

* Speakers of the Society.
† A magnificent, though bold figure. The **Red Lion** (which is the sign of the inn at which the UNION assembled), and which is a remarkably handsome lion of the kind, is described as wagging his *tail*, in testimony of the pleasure he felt at the goings on within.

II. 2.

Master of a mighty college,
   Without his robe behold him stand;
Whom not a Whig will now acknowledge,
   Return his bow, or shake his hand.
Is the sable Jackson fled?
Thy friend is gone—he hides his powder'd head.
The Bedells, too, by whom the mace is borne?
Gone to salute the rising morn.
Fair laughs the morn, and soft the zephyr blows;
   While, gently sidling through the crowded street,
In scarlet robe, Clare's * tiny master goes,
   Ware † clears the road, and Gunning† guides his feet,
Regardless of the sweeping whirlwind's sway,
   That, hush'd in green repose, marks J—mmy's for
     its prey.

II. 4.

Fill the *Audit* bowl!
   The feast in hall prepare!
'Reft of his robes, he yet may share the feast,
   Close by the master's chair.
Contempt and laughter scowl
A baneful smile upon their baffled guest.—
   Heard ye the din of battle bray,
Gown to gown, and cap to cap?
Hark at the Johnian gates each thund'ring rap,
   While through opposing Dons they move their way.
Ye Johnian towers, old W—d's eternal shame,

     * The Vice-chancellor elect.
     † Two of the Esquire Bedells.

With many a midnight imposition fed,
Revere his Algebra's immortal fame,
   And spare the meek mechanic's holy head.
Each bristled boar will bear no more,
And, meeting in the combination-room,
They stamp their vengeance deep, and ratify his doom

III. 1.

J–mmy, lo ! to sudden fate
   (Pass the wine—the liquor's good)
Half of thy year we consecrate :
   The *web* is now what was the *word*.
But mark the scene beneath the senate's height :
   See the petition's crowded skirts unroll ;
Visions of glory spark my aching sight,
   Unborn commencements crowd not on my soul.
No more our Kaye,* our Thackery,* we bewail ;
All hail ! thou genuine prince !† Brittania's issue, hail!

III. 2.

Heads of houses, doctors bold,
   Sublime the hoods and wigs they rear ;
Masters young and fellows old
   In bombazeen and silk appear ;
In the midst a form divine,—
His eye proclaims him of the British line.
What cheers of triumph thunder through the air,
   While the full tide of youthful thanks is poured !
Hear from your chambers, Price ‡ and Hibbert,‡ hear :

      * Former Vice-chancellors.
      † The Chancellor.
      ‡ Speakers of the society.

The oppressor shrinks, the UNION is restored.
The treasurer flies to spread the news he brings,
And wears, for triumph's sake, yet larger clitterings.

III. 3.

Fond impious man, think'st thou thy puny fist,
   Thy *Wood*-en sword, has broke a British club?
The treasurer soon augments our growing list,—
   We rise more numerous from this transient rub.
Enough for me: with joy I see
   The different dooms our fates assign;
Be thine contempt and big-wigg'd care,—
   To triumph, and to die, are mine."
He spoke, and headlong from the window's height,
Deep in a dung-cart near, he plunged to endless night.†

PARR.

In his youthful days, the learned doctor happened to
: present at a musical party, when a lady's MANTUA,
nfortunately, swept from the table a valuable CREMONA,
her no small consternation, and the great grief of the
usician. On this occasion, the facetious doctor made the
ippiest application of a passage of Virgil, on record:—

'MANTUA ræ! misereræ nimium vicina CREMONÆ."

† The UNION is now restored, but the discussions are
stricted to political events previous to 1800.

PORSON.

Porson being at a party, where a certain classical lec turer, of Trinity College, was ridiculed for his pronuncia tion of *nimirum* (which he pronounced *nimirum*), pro tended warmly to defend him, to the no small astonish ment of his friends; and, being asked the reason, the Greek professor, with inimitable wit, replied,—" That was by no means surprising that the learned lecturer ha erred respecting this word, for that Horace himself ha declared, in his Epistle to Claudius, that there was bi one man in the Roman Empire who really understood it

' Septimius, Claudi, *nimirum* intelligit unus.' "

THE CRAB-FISH.

The Greek professor, Porson, was very fond of crab fish, and, being at a friend's one night to sup, he int mated a wish to have his appetite indulged. This frien jocularly replied, that he should have the finest in S James's Market, if he would go thither, buy, and brin it home, himself. Porson, to his astonishment, took hi at his word, and marched through some of the gaye streets in London, with the *crab* under his arm.

CURIOUS EPITAPH.

We are confident our readers will require no apolog for our introducing a *grave* subject amongst the *facetic* when they read the following singular whim of a wel

own *Christian*.   On the death of his wife, at an ad-
nced age, he caused the following eccentric MEMENTO
ORI to be inscribed on a marble slab, placed over her
mains :—

> *Mors loquitur*.—UXOREM TENEO.
> MARITUM EXPECTO.

eath speaks.—*" I hold the wife !   Expect the husband !"*

This worthy divine, having arrived at a good old age,
s lately resigned himself into the hands of his Redeemer,
d the stone, now reversed, presents to the eye of the
quiring observer, an *unpolished* surface.—*Requiescant
pace.*

BOROUGH INTEREST.

The late Lord Sandwich, who was well known both at
ton and Cambridge by the *cognomentum* of " *Jemmy
witcher*," having the privilege of appointing a chorister
Trinity College, presented that society with one not
ly ignorant of music, but also destitute of the three es-
ntials necessary to make a singer,—*voice, taste*, and
r,—and for no other reason was he appointed, but be-
use he had a *vote* for Huntingdon.   This gave rise to
e following pointed

EPIGRAM.

A singing man, and cannot sing,—
    From whence arose your patron's bounty ?
Give us a song ?—" Excuse me, sir,
    My voice is in another county."

EXTRAORDINARY ACT IN DIVINITY.

The following curious *act in divinity*, wherein D
John Davenant was *respondent*, and Dr. Richardson
amongst others, *opponent*, was kept at Cambridge, befor
King James. The question was maintained in th
negative, concerning the *excommunicating* of kings. Di
Richardson gravely pressed the practice of St. Ambrose
who excommunicated the Emperor Theodosius, so home
that the king, in a great passion, retorted,—" *Profect
fuit hoc ab Ambrosio insolentissimè !*" To this apothegr
of his majesty, Dr. R—se joined,—" *Responsum ver
regium, et Alexandro dignum, hoc non est argumenta dis
solvere, sed dececare.*" And, sitting down, the doctor wa
silent.

PIGEON-SHOOTING.

A punning Cantab of our acquaintance, whose *dexte*
we have often *fisted*, happened to be present when tw
gents made a match to shoot pigeons. The conversatioı
turned on the choice of the breed, and one of the bettoı
named the *blue-rock*, as the best,—" They may be so,
observed our friend Cantab, " but, were I going to shoot
I should choose *tumblers !*"

SIR ISAAC NEWTON.

The following incidents are highly characteristic of th
above recondite and celebrated Cantab, and show a
amiable simplicity of manners, though an utter disregar

t.

of worldly affairs, so much was he ever absorbed in his beloved philosophical pursuits. It is said, that Sir Isaac set out in life a professed and clamorous *infidel*, but that, on a close examination of the evidences of Christianity, he found reason, nor did he disdain, to retract his opinion. When the celebrated Dr. Edmund Halley was one day talking infidelity before him, Sir Isaac exclaimed,—" Man, you had better hold your tongue : you are talking about what you do not understand." So patient was this great man, not only in his pursuit of truth, but also in suffering under pain, that when, in his last illness, that of the stone, his agony was so great, that drops of sweat forced themselves through a double night-cap, which he wore, he never was heard to complain or cry out. Sir Isaac had a *prism* sent him from abroad, by a philosophical friend, which was at that time a very scarce commodity in England ; and, being desired to say what the value of it was, by the custom-house officers, that they might be able to regulate the duty to be paid, the great man, whose business was more with the universe than with duties and drawbacks, rated the prism according to his own idea of its utility, and answered,—" Its value was so great, he could not ascertain it." Being again pressed for an estimate, he persisted in his former reply, and the result was, that he paid an exorbitant duty for what might have been taken away by paying a rate according to the simple weight of the glass. At another time, a favourite little dog, named Diamond, having, in his absence, entered his study, he found it, on his return, diverting itself with the remains of some valuable MSS., containing the *memoranda* of many years' laborious research, which it had already torn into a thousand pieces; but so great a com-

and had this genius over his temper, that, gathering up
ie remnants, he patted the offender on the head, saying,
—" O ! Diamond, Diamond, you know not what mis-
nief you have done ?"

THE MODERN PONTIUS PILATE.

What Cantab has not heard of the Modern Pontius
'ilate ? Such was the designation of a late celebrated
ivine of King's College, who was wont to boast of his
xtraordinary powers in the *wordy* race; protesting that
ie would give any man as far as *Pontius Pilate* in the
Apostolic Creed, and beat him hollow before he came to
' AMEN !"—Qu.* *amens!* as it appears from the reverend
entleman's own confession, that he was *plural* in his
ronunciation; for, on being asked how he could accom-
lish it, he declared he could pronounce *three* words at
once.

TIT-BITS.

The celebrated author of *The Diversions of Purley*,
Home Tooke, being once invited especially to meet his
no less celebrated brother Cantab, Dr. Parr, exclaimed,
on receiving the message,—" What, go to meet a country schoolmaster; a mere man of Greek and Latin
scraps! that will never do." Some time after, the former meeting the latter gentleman in the street, he went
up to the doctor, and addressed him with—" Ah! my
dear Parr, is it you? How gratified I am to see you."—

* *Scilicet*, dementated, alias downright *mad*.

L 2

" What, me?" replied Parr, " a mere country school-master; a man of Greek and Latin scraps!"—" Oh, my good friend," rejoined Horne Tooke, with his accustomed promptitude of wit, " those who told you that never understood me; when I spoke of the *scraps*, I meant the *tit-bits!*"

A FORCIBLE ARGUMENT.

That erudite Cantab, Bishop Burnett, preaching before Charles II., being much warmed with his subject, uttered some religious truth with great vehemence, and, at the same time, striking his fist on the desk with great violence, cried out,—" Who dare deny this?"—" Faith," said the king, in a tone more *piano* than that of the orator, " nobody that is within the reach of that fist of your's."

REFORM EXTRAORDINARY.

The men of Maudlin College, Cambridge, had been long celebrated for their wineless lives, and a bowl of BISHOP or *milk-punch*, or a COPUS of AUDIT ale, would have been, to their νους-less heads, both a bane and antidote: like Dr. Johnson, they would sip their TEA, even to the sixteenth cup. At length, one of the society resolved to root out this *spirit*-less propensity, and redeem the credit of his college; and he endeavoured to effect this reform extraordinary in the following extraordinary manner;—having invited to his rooms ten or twelve of the most inveterate *tea-discussers*, he took a *bottle and a half* of wine from a sideboard, and then, placing himself with his back against the door, he flourished the poker

over his head, declaring, in very emphatic terms,——
" That not a soul of them should depart till every drop
of the *wine* was drunk !" Whether this experiment had
the immediate desired effect, we cannot say, but this we
know, that they no longer labour under the tea-drinking
imputation.

CHANTING À-LA-GREEK.

During the time that the erudite Dr. Bentley was pre-
paring an edition of Homer, which he had undertaken at
the desire of Earl Grenville, he was accustomed not unfrequently to spend his evenings with that distinguished
nobleman. These congenials, when drinking deep at
the classic fountain, would sometimes keep it up to a
late hour. One morning, after one of their mental ca-
rousals, the mother of his lordship reproached him for
keeping the *country clergyman*, as she termed the learned
Cantab, till he was *intoxicated*. Lord Grenville denied
the charge,——on which the lady replied, he could not
have sung in so ridiculous a manner, if he had not been
in *liquor ;* but the truth was, that the singing, which appeared so to have annoyed the noble lady, was no other
than the doctor endeavouring to entertain and instruct
Lord Grenville in the true *catilena,* or *recitative,* of the
ancients.

DR. SAMUEL CLARKE *versus* THE REGIUS PROFESSOR OF DIVINITY.

When that profound scholar and divine, Dr. Samuel
Clarke, deemed it necessary for him to proceed to the degree of D.D., he entered the schools, in Cambridge,

with the two following questions, as the basis of his *public
exercise;* and the manner in which this erudite Cantab
acquitted himself, is worthy of being handed down to
the latest posterity :—

I. *Nullum fidei Christianæ dogma, in S. Scripturis
traditum, est rectæ rationi dissenteneum.*

II. *Sine actionum humanarum libertate nulla potest
esse religio.*

1. *No article of the Christian faith, delivered in the
Holy Scriptures, is disagreeable to right reason.*

2. *Without the liberty of human actions, there can be
no religion.*

These two *questions* were worthy of such a divine and
philosopher, to propose for a *public debate.*   Dr. James
was the Regius Professor, a learned and very acute dis-
putant, and he exerted himself beyond his accustomed
practice, in order to oppose and try Dr. Clarke to the utmost.   Possessed of a retentive memory, and fluent in
words, with a natural turn for disputation, the professor
began with an *examination* of the candidate's *thesis* (an
elaborate discourse founded on the first question), sifting
every part with the strictest nicety, and pressed him with
all the force of *syllogistic argument.*   He was an *adversary*
worthy of the *respondent,* who made an *extempore* reply
to the learned professor's *queries,* which occupied nearly
half an hour, without hesitation ; and with such perspi-
cuity of *thought* and purity of *language* did he *take off* all
that the professor had advanced against his opinions,
that those who heard him were astonished thereat, and
declared that, had they not seen him, they should have
supposed his *reply* to have been previously written.   He

guarded so well, replied so readily and clearly, and pressed so close upon the professor, in his replies through the remainder of the disputation, that perhaps such a conflict, kept up with such spirit, and which ended with such perfect honour to the *respondent*, was never before heard in the *schools*. The professor, who was a man of humour as well as learning, after a long *disputation*, used often to say to a respondent,—" *Finem jam faciem, nam te probè exercui* ;" (I will now make an end, for I have sufficiently worked you). He was about to address the same words to Dr. Clarke ; but, after the word *te*, he stopped and corrected himself, by saying,— " *Nam ME probè* EXERCUISTI," (for *you* have worked ME thoroughly); a high compliment, in his humorous way of expressing himself: but so justly did Dr. Clarke merit it, that those who heard the *disputation* declared that, for handling his argument, the fluency and (notwithstanding his great attention to other matters) purity of his *Latinity*, he spoke as one who had discoursed in no other language, and was an ornament to the university.

ADVICE GRATIS.

At the sittings of Guildhall, an action of debt was tried, before Lord Mansfield, in which the defendant, a merchant of London, with great warmth, complained of the plaintiff's conduct, to his lordship, in having caused him to be arrested, not only in the face of the day, but in the Royal Exchange, and in the face of the whole assembled credit of the metropolis. The chief justice stopped him with great composure, saying,—" Friend, you forget yourself; *you* were the *defaulter*, in refusing to pay a

just debt: and let me give you a piece of advice worth
more to you than the debt and costs : be careful not to
put it in any man's power to arrest you, either in public
or private, for the future."

THE BRIDE IN WAITING.

A celebrated Cantab, who, for his poetic taste and
splendid imagination, might almost be designated the
" ANGEL OF THE WORLD," had the *good* fortune to lead
to the altar of Hymen a blooming bride, and the *misfortune*, amidst his angelic speculations, to forget her. The
happy pair were to start for Paris, to spend the honey-
moon, immediately after the ceremony ; the bridegroom
begged an hour to *pack* for the occasion,—the smiling
fair one granted his request,—the hour was past, but he
did not appear ; two, three, four, five hours, which, to
the lady, were as many ages, had Sol laboured towards
the western horizon, and she was still in waiting. A
messenger was despatched in search of the truant, and
Paris was found, not as many Cantabs are, in the midst
of triangles, &c. but, forgetful of his Helen, rearing a
temple to the muses, totally unconscious of the part he
had so lately acted in the consummation of holy matri-
mony.

BON MOT.

" The Bishop of London," says Aubrey, " having cut
down a noble *cloud* of trees at Fulham, Lord Chancellor
Bacon told him, ' he was a good expounder of *dark*
places.' "

DR. HENNIKER'S DEFINITION OF WIT.

Dr. Henniker being one day in conversation with that celebrated statesman, the Earl of Chatham, amongst other questions, was asked, by his lordship, how he defined wit?—" Wit," replied the learned doctor, " is like what a pension would be given by your lordship to your humble servant,—a good thing well applied."

WHAT A DEBAUCH!

A pious queen's-man being invited to a *spread*, refused the *invite*, on the ground of the last evening's excesses,— when, upon being pressed to tell when and how he had spent the previous night, he, with reluctance, confessed he had committed a *great debauch*, inasmuch as he had sat up till ten o'clock, and drank *two bumpers of plum wine ! ! Silicet*, raisin.

NEW READINGS.

Every son of Alma Mater has, *a primis ephebis*, appropriated to his own schoolmates the humorous translation of the words—*coctilibus muris*, by cocktailed mice; and not a few have thought that the *arma virumque cano Trojæ qui primus ab oris*, alluded to the archididascalus, with his cane for his arms, and his mouth as prim as a Trojan's ; but we much question whether the sense of a Latin writer was ever more ludicrously misunderstood, than in the lecture-room of Christ College, when a deep-read freshman rendered the words—"*anteponit tenuem victum copioso*," (he prefers a slender diet to an abundant one), by " he places before them a thin man conquered by a stout one," which, when we consider that our author was alluding to the manners and customs of the gladiators, must cause a smile.

EPIGRAMS.

I.

Had thy spouse, Dr. Drumstick, been ta'en from thy
    side,
In the same way that Eve became Adam's fair bride,
And again by thy side on the bridal bed laid ;
Though thou couldst not, like Adam, have gallantly said
"Thou art flesh of my flesh,"—because flesh thou hast
    none,
Thou with truth mighst have said—"Thou art bone of
    my bone."

II.

On the Marriage of a very thin Couple.

St. Paul has declared that, when persons, though twain,
Are in wedlock united, one flesh they remain.
But had he been by, when, like Pharoah's kine pairing,
Dr. D—gl-s, of B—n—t, espoused Miss M—nw-r-ng,
The apostle, no doubt, would have alter'd his tone,
And have said, " These two splinters shall now make
    one bone."

III.

On a Petit-Maitre Physician.

When P-nn-ngt-n for female ills indites,
Studying alone not what, but how he writes,
The ladies, as his graceful form they scan,
Cry, with ill-omen'd rapture—" *Killing man !*"

IV.

On a Student being put out of Commons, for missing Chapel.

To fast and pray we are by Scripture taught :
O could I do but either as I ought !
In both, alas ! I err ; my frailty such—
I pray too little, and I fast too much.

PARODIES ON COLLEGE EXAMINATIONS.

As we commenced the " Facetiæ " with a satirical imi
tation of a college examination-paper, we have intro
duced three more, from different sources, to wind up
this part of the volume.

EXAMINATION I.

1. Prove, by syllogistic ratiocination, that chalk and
cheese are not one and the same thing—that they are no

idem in genere; and then render an analytical exposition of the composition of chalk, and a disquisition synthetical on that of cheese. Show, further, which of these two kinds of exposition it is probable Aristotle would have adopted in treating such a subject.

2. Demonstrate by induction why it is, that, in his expedition into India, Alexander Magnus followed his nose.

3. Give the definition of China pig—nominally, accidentally, physically, and metaphysically.

4. Convert the two first books of Aristotle's Treatise on Rhetoric into Latin hexameter and pentameter, and the third and fourth books of the Annals of Tacitus into pindarics.

5. Are you anywhere informed by Herodotus, which were the thickest, the heads of the Egyptians or the Persians?

6. Make a computation of the probable thickness of the eads of both nations; and then logically demonstrate the difference of inches in the skulls of one and the other.

7. Give the Greek appellations of the several terms—tea, coffee, snuff, and tobacco—printer's devil, leather-breeches-maker, steam-packet, double-barrelled gun—tag, rag, and bobtail.

8. Why is it probable that Horace, if he could have gotten them, would have worn spectacles?—What was his height without his shoes?—Signify the colour of his complexion by two tropes, one metaphor, and three similes.

9. Prove the non-identity of Sylla the dictator and Scylla the sand-bank; and does not the sea or C make all the difference between them?

10. Translate the following passage from Tag's Ode to Miss Pickle, into a Sapphic stanza, both in Greek and Latin :—

" Not pickled onion, nor yet pickled bean,
 Nor pickled cabbage, either red or green,
 Nor pickled cucumber, nor pickled Chili,
 But my own darling little Picklelilly."

11. Oxford must, from all antiquity, have been either somewhere or nowhere. Where was it in the time of Tarquinius Priscus? If it was nowhere, it surely must have been somewhere. Where was it?

12. Should you, upon consideration, say that the ancients could find the way to their mouths in the dark as well as the moderns? Do you believe the Athenians wore Wellington-boots, or ate mince-pies at Christmas.

13. Mention any instances that occur to you of ancients visiting any part of the United States. Are we not to infer, from the frequent occurrence of the word γας in their most celebrated authors, that the Athenians were perfectly acquainted with that valuable commodity?

14. Trace the derivation of pump from πυς, according to the example afforded you of that of bump from βυς.— Βυς, Ionicè Βοος, per apocopen Βος, poetic Βυς, per pepper-castor Βυπ, and per epenthesin Βυμπ, hence you may easily trace the derivation of pumpkin and bumpkin.

15. State logically how many tails a cat has.

From these specimens, however much he may admire the erudition they display, the reader will, perhaps, not think very favourably of the utility of university examinations, but useful they are. The answers would occupy

o much space ; suffice it, therefore, to say, our com-
municant got off with flying colours, the delight of his
connections, and an honour to his house.   The answer
to the last question, however, amused us so much that
we cannot refrain from giving it.

15. State logically how many tails a cat has ?—Ans.
Cats have three tails—no cat has two tails—every cat has
one tail more than no cat—*ergo*, every cat has three
tails.

EXAMINATION II.

1. Give a comparative sketch of the principal English theatres, with the dates of their erection, and the
names of the most eminent candle-snuffers at each. What
were the stage-boxes ? What were the offices of promp-
ter—ballet-master—and scene-shifter?   In what part
of the theatre was the one-shilling gallery ? Distinguish
accurately between operas and puppet-shows.

2. Where was Downing Street ? Who was prime-
minister when Cribb defeated Molineux—and where
did the battle take place ? Explain the terms milling
—fibbing—cross buttock—neck and crop—bang up—
and—prime.

3. Give the dates of all the parliaments, from their
first institution to the period of the hard frost on the
Thames. In what month of what year was Mr. Abbot
elected speaker? Why was he called *" the little man in
the wig?"* When the speaker was out of the chair, where
was the mace put?

4. Enumerate the principal houses of call in and about
London, marking those of the tailors, bricklayers, and
shoemakers, and stating from what brewery each house

was supplied with brown stout. Who was the tutelary saint of the shoemakers? At what time was his feast celebrated? Who was St. Swithin? Do you remember any remarkable English proverb respecting him?

5. Give a ground-plan of Gilead House. Mention the leading topics of the Guide to Health, with some account of the Anti-Impetigines—Daffy's Elixir—Blaine's Distemper Powders—Ching's Worm Lozenges—and Hooper's Female Pills.

6. Give characters of Wat Tyler, Jack Cade, and Sir Francis Burdett. Did the latter return from the Tower by water or land? On what occasion did Mr. Lethbridge's "hair stand on *ind?*" Correct the solecism, and give the reason of your alteration.

7. Enumerate the roads on which double toll was taken on the Sundays. Did this custom extend to Christmas Day and Good Friday? Who was toll-taker at Tyburn when Mrs. Brownrigg was executed?

8. Distinguish accurately between sculls and oars—boat and punt—jackass and donkey—gauger, exciseman, and supervisor—pantaloons, trousers, gaiters, and overalls.—At what place of education were any of these forbidden? Which? and Why?

9. Express the following words in the Lancashire, Derbyshire, London, and Exmoor dialects:—bacon—poker—you—I—doctor—and turnpike-gate.

10. Mention the principal coach-inns in London, with a correct list of the coaches which set out from the Bolt-in-Tun. Where were the chief stands of hackney coaches,—and what was the No. of that in which the Princess Charlotte drove to Connaught House? To what stand do you suppose this removed after it set her down?

11. Give a succinct account, with dates, of the following persons—Belcher—Mr. Waithman—Major Cart-
wright—Martin Van Butchell—and Edmund Henry
Barker.

12. Draw a map of the Thames with the surrounding
country, marking particularly Wapping, Blackwall,
Richmond, and the Isle of Dogs. Distinguish between
Newcastle-on-Tyne, and Newcastle-under-Line—Gloucester and Double Gloucester—and the two Richmonds.
What celebrated teacher flourished at one of them ?—and
who were his most eminent disciples?

13. What were the various sorts of paper in use amongst
the English ? To what purpose was *whited-brown* chiefly
applied ? What was size? Distinguish between this
and college Sizings, and state the ordinary expense of pa-
pering a room.

14. " For every one knows little *Matt.'s* an M. P."
Frag. Com. Inc. ap. Morn. Chron. vol. 59, p. 1624.

What reasons can you assign for the general knowledge of this fact? Detail, at length, the ceremony of
chairing a member. What were the hustings? Who
paid for them? Explain the abbreviations—Matt. M. P.
—Tom—Dick—F.R.S.—L.L.D.—and A.S.S.

15. What was the distinguishing title of the mayors
of London ? Did any other city share the honour? Give
a list of the mayors of London from Sir Richard Whit-
ington to Sir William Curtis, with an account of the
fat of the first, and the weight of the last. What is
meant by Lord Mayor's Day? Describe the *Apotheca-
ies'* barge, and give some account of marrow-bones and
cleavers.

16. When was Spyring and Marsden's Lemon Acid

ivented? Distinguish between this and Essential Salt
f Lemons. Enumerate the principal patentees, espe-
ially those of liquid blacking.

17. Scan the following lines—

> But for shaving and tooth-drawing,
> Bleeding, cabbaging, and sawing,
> Dicky Gossip, Dicky Gossip is the man!

What is known of the character and history of Dicky
Gossip?

EXAMINATION III.

1. Find the centre of gravity in a leg of mutton, and
determine with precision how much gravy it ought to
contain when properly cooked. Is there any difference
between a leg and a shoulder? and what? Is it not an
anomaly to call the fore-leg of a sheep the shoulder? and
in what London market did the absurdity originate?

2. Describe the difference between a jack-ass and a
jack-fish; and enumerate the various kinds of jack-asses
that are to be found in and about the university.

3. Give an account of the Olympic games, and point
out the resemblance that there is between them and the
Olympic Theatre in Wych Street. What street is Wych
Street, and which is the way to it?

4. In what part of London are there the greatest number of fools? and *vice versá*. Are the knaves in office
more annoying than the knaves out of office? and, if not,
why not? Give the characters respectively of a lord
mayor, a merry-Andrew, a prime minister, a bishop,
and a quack doctor. Mark the difference, if any, between them, and show in what they are all just alike.

M

5. Where was Cribb when the battle of Waterloo was fought; and who was the real champion of England on that memorable day?

6. Enumerate the various qualities of Henry Hunt's Matchless Blacking, his Roasted Corn, and his quondam friend Cobbett's History of the Reformation. Analyse the three, and say which should be taken internally, and which applied externally, and why?

7. Give an account of the Epping Hunt on an Easter Monday, and explain the reason why the horses generally go a great many more miles than their riders; also, why the cockneys so often indulge in their propensity for stag-hunting, when it is notorious that they are themselves properly classed under the head of horned animals in the best treatises on natural history.

8. Determine what it was that Peeping Tom of Coventry wished to see. Having found that out, ascertain whether the rays from that focus of attraction were too dazzling for his optic nerves, or whether excessive straining of his eyeballs occasioned his blindness?

9. Give the diameter, and then find the circumference, of Mr. Green's new balloon. Having correctly ascertained these, show why Miss Stocks was found on her back and Mr. Harris on his face when they so unfortunately, and fatally for H., descended near Croydon. Determine, also, whether it was on the principle of expansion or compression that the accident took place, and how many feet distant from the earth the aeronauts were when Miss Stocks put the glass of brandy to her lips.

10. Name the principal banking-houses in London, and give a general description of all the parish beadles within the bills of mortality. Repeat the observations

nade by Sir Richard Birnie to Michael O'Shaunessy, the
cobbler, when he was taken to Bow Street for making a
ap-stone of his wife's head. Show the connection be-
ween each of these propositions, and say in what parti-
culars they vary.

11. Why should Harriette Wilson, Miss Foote, and
he Princess Olive be considered of more consequence
han ladies of quality generally? What qualities do
adies of quality generally possess? and what is the dif-
erence between a lady of rank and a rank lady?

12. Where is Covent Garden situate, and what flow-
rs thrive best there? Upon what principle is it that the
productions reared in the neighbourhood of this celebrated garden delight in hot beds, and yet come to ma-
urity without being forced?

13. Where did Parson Irving come from before he
ame from Scotland, and where is he likely to go to if he
continues to go on in the way he is going? Determine
how nearly he is related to Dr. Eady, and what degree
of affinity subsists between them and the Rev. Alexander Fletcher?

14. What is the difference between a dentist, a den-
ist-surgeon, and a tooth-drawer? Which of these is the
Chevalier Ruspini, which Dr. Bew, of Brighton, and
which Mr. Hartrey, of Hayes Court? Show that the two
former are entitled to a guinea, although the last receives
only a shilling per tooth, in consequence of the infinitely
greater trouble they take in the performance of their task!

15. Describe the different kinds of breeches that are at
present worn by the English. Name the tailor that made
he first pair, and determine with accuracy how much
nore double-milled kerseymere it takes to make a pair

of Wellington trousers for Lord Nugent than would be necessary for the Achilles in Hyde Park.

16. What reasons can you assign for the necessity of having one leg or the other always foremost when walking ! and, having proved that a man can step a yard at a time, ascertain how far he can reach in a hop, step, and a jump.

17. Scan the following lines, and then translate them into Latin hexameters :

> " High diddle diddle !
> The cat and the fiddle,
> The cow jumped over the moon !"

In what quarter was the moon when the cow jumped over her ? Was it an Alderney or a Welsh cow ? State, also, whether she descended on her legs after her extraordinary leap, and in what parish she fell.

18. When was April Fool's-Day first observed ? Who is the first April fool upon record ? What city had the honour of inventing bug-traps ? Of what size were the fleas which Sir Joseph Banks mistook for lobsters, and how much salt did he put in the saucepan, when he boiled them ? If one flea can skip a mile in an hour, in what time would a million of fleas draw the mail-coach from London to Bath ?

19. Enumerate the different figures of speech made use of by the late Lord Londonderry, and state precisely what sort of figure his lordship cut, when he stood prostrate before the House, and spoke of his fundamental features ? Where was Mr. Canning at that time ? What honourable member was it that turned his back upon himself, and in what manner did he effect so novel a position?

Cambridge Parties:

BY

TWO DISTINGUISHED CANTABS.

(Originally printed in the Brighton Magazine.)

CAMBRIDGE PARTIES,

&c. &c.

LETTER I.

WATER-PARTIES.

DEAR ———,—There is no period of a man's existence,
it is generally observed, to which, in the retrospection of
days gone by, he recurs with such peculiar feelings of satisfaction, as the three years passed at the university:—
often, amid the troubles and vexations of maturer life,
will he sigh to reflect upon the times when his whole
cares, if cares he had, consisted in rising on a cold frosty
morning for lectures, learning an imposition for the proc-
tors, or leaving a wine-party for chapel; and I doubt
whether (unless in the felicitous era of the honey-moon)
he would not joyfully resign his present prospects, could
he once more, with cap and gown, take his place among
the undergraduates of the university. As a memento,
therefore, of past happiness, and showing the difference
of what was, and what is, I have thought that " Letters
from Cambridge," elucidating its present manners and
customs, *would* be interesting to you, and *might* be to
others; at any rate I shall amuse myself, and with us,
you know, amusement is a main object.

You will think a description of " Water-Parties," at this time of the year, a curious commencement of my correspondence; but the fact is, that, owing to the late extreme mildness of the weather, they have been more frequent during this last month than at any former period of my residence. Both from the pleasure I have formerly enjoyed in them with you, and from being well assured they are parties which give the most favourable idea of Cambridge character and Cambridge manners, I have resolved to commence with them. At *breakfast-parties*, some men are not quite awake; with others, the thoughts of lectures intrude; at *wine-parties*, reserve is not always thrown off till the wine has begun to take effect; and, at *supper-parties*, " *I must be in before twelve, or I shall be hauled up before the master;*"—" *I must go home to prepare for lectures;*"—" *I'm d——d sleepy;*"— " *Well, good night, old boy! I must get up early to-morrow, to hunt;*"—are continually grating upon our ears, and marring our comfort. But in *water-parties* there is no drawback of this sort. The men who form it are in general well acquainted, have a day of comparative idleness before them (in itself peculiarly pleasant, by the by), and are previously resolved to be social and jolly; to blow care to the winds; to *be* happy; and, as far as they can, to *make* happy.

Under the influence of such feelings, a party of us, consisting of S—, K—, and G—, of Christ's College; H—, of Clare; B—, of Pembroke; C—, of Jesus; I—, of Trinity, and myself, sallied out on one of the finest days of last week, to man the *Glory*, a six-oared boat of Cross's. It was a most lovely morning,—

" The sun was in the heavens, and joy on earth."

Few of us, I believe, thought much about the sun, but "the joy on earth" we *felt*; though, like Lambro, we were not philosophers enough to stop and inquire the reason. As we rowed in a leisurely way down the stream, this joy was manifested in various ways, by various characters. B— gave vent to his feelings in a poetical effusion:—

> " Once more upon the waters—yet once more—
> And the waves bound beneath me, like a steed
> That knows its rider."

Lord Byron was now handed from one to the other in very fine style; from K—, G—, and I—, I remarked, among others, the following strains :—

K—." How gloriously her gallant course she goes !
*   *   *   *

> She walks the waters like a thing of life,
> And seems to dare the elements to strife.
> Who would not brave the battle-fire—the wreck—
> To move the monarch of her peopled deck ?"

G—." Oh ! who can tell, save he whose heart hath tried,
> And danc'd in triumph o'er the waters wide*,
> The exulting sense—the pulse's maddening play,
> That thrills the wanderer of that trackless way ?"

We could see, by the shrewd mathematical face with which H— was regarding the blade of his oar, that any thing but poetry occupied *his* attention ; he was, in fact, enumerating the number of strokes given in " t"; and

---

* Not over wide, by the by.

the newly acquired velocity after each impulse. C—
was rather offended at his observing, he had found it, on
calculation, pretty much the same whether C— pulled
or not.

S— began to spout Virgil; but this was voted a bore,
as there were one or two in the company who might not
understand it. For my part, I moralized; but had got
no farther than " immortal man," when my meditations
were interrupted by an " unhallowed sound" of singing.
S—, determined not to be outdone in noise, had got hold
of the poor Canadian boat-song, and was giving tongue
most gloriously in conjunction with C—, and, therefore,
lending my assistance, we came the " row" part both
with arms and voices very gaily.

Loud was the laughter after each effusion, and numberless the jests which were passed; I should like to
transcribe some of these for your edification, but, unfortunately, I am not quite sure they would have so good
an appearance in print. Our feelings were then very un-
critical. A bad pun may create a laugh, and a good
one could do no more; however, this must be the subject of a future paper, and lo! while I am tarrying with
you, our boat has arrived at Chesterton locks.

* " *Here, S—, you Christian son of a gun! Come and*

---

* You and others may complain that, in the dialogues or
exclamations, here and elsewhere inserted, there is neither
wit, delicacy, nor elegance. To this I can only answer, that
a conversation, composed of these ingredients, would seem
either pedantic, or inconsistent with the characters of Cam-
bridgemen. As this is a most true account of the party, and
I have inserted nothing which did not actually occur, neither would I put down an exclamation that was not actually made.

apply your fat carcass to this lock." "That's your sort.
" T——, take care of that oar, and pull it out of the ru
lucks." "Here, give me the boat-hook, and keep off th
side." "By jingo, here's F——." "Verily, I'm astound
ed." "Why, F——, my little minimum! What the plagu
can have brought you from your sines and cosines, to com
rambling upon this ' wide wide sea?' You're reading hy
drostatics, I suppose, and want to take a practical observa
tion of the motions of bodies and fluids!——Well! Mind yo
don't make a practical illustration *of it; for sometim*
these said bodies will find the bottom, you know." "Yo
impudent thief! n'importe, ' il rit bien qui rit le dernier
I prophesy you'll be heartily sick of your motions, at lea
those of the oar, before you get far; for if you look fo
ward you will observe a party in the Stag, resting on the
oars, and waiting, in order to give you the benefit of a goo
sweating—so look to it." "The Devil they are! come, m
boys, have a regard to your characters." "H——, give th
stroke." "That will do." "Good-by, professor." "G
it." "Now we are even." "Incumbite remis."

> " Away we go, and what care we
>   For tumults, treasons, or for wars;
>   We are as calm in our delight,
>   As is the crescent moon so bright
>   Amid the scatter'd stars !"

Not quite so calm, though, either! I must own,
soon began, as F—— predicted, to grow weary of thes
quick motions, and would rather have been meditatin
upon the fine effect with Lord Byron, than partaking i
this calm and gentle exercise :——

" By he avens it is a splendid sight to see
(For one who hath no part—no fagging there),
The rival coats of mix'd embroidery,
The oars which glitter in the sun's bright glare ;
How gallantly the boatsmen bend and rise,
And bend again, loud yelling in the race," &c.

Having kept together, boat and boat, for upwards of a mile, some fears came across me that we might go on *ad infinitum,*—and, feeling that my strength would not proceed in the same ratio, I thought proper to give a few small hints on the subject of dropping the contest. " *I think we are great asses for thus fagging ourselves.*" No corresponding effect; the men determined to be asses. " *It's a devilish ungentlemanly thing to sweat ourselves in this manner, like bargemen!*" All in vain. " *Hang it, T—, you've got no pluck ; pull away, my hearty !*" On we went, at the rate of at least twenty miles an hour, all for glory, when, fortunately for me, just at this critical time, a poor wight in a canoe, who, I dare say, thought it every wit as ungentlemanly as I did to row so fast, unable to clear both boats in time, was very neatly run down by us. There were really many of our party who were so inhumane as to wish to leave him to sink or swim ; but I very magnanimously prevailed upon them to row back to his assistance. It was a long time before we could persuade the poor fellow he was not drowned ; and, when this was effected, he was so pleased, that he forgot to row us for upsetting him, but seemed half inclined to thank us for the honour we had done him. I doubt not, though, that, when he came to himself, he would begin to question the propriety of our conduct, and send a few blessings after us. Uninjured by these, we gallantly pursued our course, although the Stag was too much a-head to give us hopes of overtaking it. It was safe now to exclaim,—" *How very unfortunate ! we were just beating them ! blow our friend of the canoe !*" Nor were any of us at all sparing of such exclamations. We could gain from the burden of our antagonist's song, that they modestly ascribed to their boat the honour of victory :—

> " Merrily, merrily, goes the bark !
> Before the gale she bounds ;
> So bounds the dolphin from the shark,
> Or the *deer* before the hounds."

Now our boat had already *glory* enough. We, therefore, thought proper to assume the present merit to our selves ; and, as the staggites did not seem inclined to raise the " io triumphè" of victory, we lifted up our voices in the famous boat-song from the Lady of the Lake :—

> " Hark to the chief who in triumph advances,
> Honour'd and bless'd be the evergreen pine," &c.

After " p" strokes (where p is very small), we bore down majestically upon Backsbite, and arrived " t" after our opponents. They of the Stag, having eyed us askance a bit, passed through the locks, while we remained stationary to feed.

The beauty of the River Cam at this point is of that species which is, in general, peculiar to the rivers of a flat country, in their departure from the haunts of men, and approach to the immeasurable main. Although Backsbite is only three miles and-a-half distant from

Cambridge, it is yet sufficiently remote to have lost its more civilized features, and to have approached to the wild and fenny beauty of sea-propinquity. For the last mile, in approaching Backsbite, little more meets the eye than beds of osiers on one bank, and an almost interminable waste on the other, broken occasionally by willows, which seem heartily tired of their situation; or by a village church in the distance, which does not inspire the same feeling, only because it is connected with better things; and which, " as it points evermore with its silent finger to heaven," resembles a beacon-fire in a storm, or an ark in the waters. In spring, however, when this waste hath acquired a yellow mantle*, and the osier beds a green one, the scene is far from being devoid of attraction. I am very much inclined to think it was the striking appearance of these osiers at one point in the river, which first suggested Lord Byron's comparison in the " Bride of Abydos :"—

> " As the stream late conceal'd
>   By the fringe of the willows,
>   When it rushes reveal'd
>   In the light of its billows;
>   As the bolt bursts on high
>   From the black cloud that bound it,
>   Flash'd the soul of that eye
>   Through the long lashes round it."

In front of a house of public entertainment which

---

* The fens appear quite yellow in spring, from the quantity of cowslips, buttercups, &c. which spring up with the turf.

stands on Backsbite locks, is a small paddock where the snobs assemble to regale themselves in summer, and which, till the dinner we had brought with us was prepared, was destined to form the theatre of our gambols. It was not difficult to find an amusement for men determined to be amused; in a moment we were all engaged in exhibiting our agility at leap-frog, or in leaping the bar; and soon after in a game of quoits for the damage of the party.

There are some who might perhaps smile with contempt at the idea of a party of young men amusing themselves by playing at leap-frog, but there are also others who would consider this very circumstance as a natural exemplification of joyful feelings that would not be controlled. Those would merely look to the agility of limb; these—to " the freshness of the heart!"

I fancy that you are at this place about exclaiming with Sir P. Teazle, " Oh, damn your sentiment." And my companions, indeed, having just concluded their game, are making such a confounded noise, that, if I wish any dinner, I must lay this aside at present and attend them.

" Huzza—Regular case of floor!"

" I say B—, how are you off for dinner? damn the expense!"

" Holloa, you chap! is dinner ready?" " Yes, sir."

" Then devil take the hindmost."

I should protract this letter to a most unconscionable length, were I to relate how much we ate, laughed, and talked. I will thank you, therefore, to imagine whatever you please (so that it be good), and to suppose us once more re-embarking in the Glory.

" Now then!—off she goes." " Go your rigs, my

boys." And as, with a cigar in my mouth, I had just quietly taken my place at the helm, I was no longer backward in exhortations and reprobations of their laziness; but roared out,—" *Row, brothers, row, the stream runs fast,"* till their ears, or at least my lungs, were heartily tired. In our progress up the stream, our boat, to a spectator from the bank, must have had a remarkably fine effect. Owing, I suppose, to the wine and malt (whose potency was so visible upon some, that G—— and S—— invariably missed the water), the crabs and backslidings were so infinite, that it must have been confidently imagined we were impelled by a small steam-engine, of which I was chimney; and that the oars were merely put out for the sake of the picturesque. And thus the ludicrous appearance was somewhat the same as that of Leporello in Don Giovanni, who mechanically moves his limbs in the action of swimming, although he is, in reality, carried along on *terra firma.*

Having advanced at the rate of a mile in three quarters of an hour, we overtook a long string of barges, which, after the fashion in this county, were towed up the stream by two or three horses, with the appropriate animals upon them, leaving a complement of four or five men to manage the craft. As they kept the middle of the river, and left us little space for the use of our oars, we vainly made several attempts to stem the current which ran violently by their side, and to shoot before their long file. Now, Cambridge-men, be it known, are mightily fond of having their own way*. Some irascible feelings

* N. B. This feature of character is generally perceptible in *undergraduates*, only when they are in the right. But some of them, when they grow older,—for instance, when

were, therefore, I am compelled to say, made manifes
upon the occasion. As to myself, as I make it a rul
never to be in a passion, I mightily enjoyed the contras
of fire on one side, and ice on the other. Here, one ol
bargee, without deigning to attend to us, busily employe
himself in haranguing his horses in the bargee lingo
which I'll be hanged if any but the brute animals coul
ever understand. Another, with a face of the most im
perturbable calmness, was leaning upon the tiller, an
staring as he smoked his pipe, with the greatest uncon
cern, both at us and our efforts ; a third, in reply to ou
swearing and blustering, derided us with " *dom it, yo*
don't pool,—pool away." Cambridge blood could bea
no more ; rhetoric was vain, and patience vainer; th
barges were boarded and the helm usurped, and, as the
were so impudent as to aver they were the better steerers
we were under the disagreeable necessity of cutting thei
ropes, and then left them, flattering ourselves we ha
effectually roused them from their lethargic calmness
and reversed the fire and ice. I will not say that a blac
eye or so was not the consequence of this skirmish, bu
this only served to enhance the pleasure; it sobere
some, and roused others; so that, in the midst of jests c
" black eyes and rainbows," &c. all in the Byronit
style, we proceeded at a very respectable rate toward
Cambridge.

It was half-past five, and some of the chapel bells wer
ringing, as we arrived at Barnwell Pool, which is di
tant half a mile from the university. It might hav

they become fellows, &c. are not very particular about th
right or wrong, but will have their way, because, as Lor
B. says, they may.

seemed, to a casual observer, that our feelings were now pretty much the same as at our passing the same spot some hours before; but there were also some minuter shades from which a different result might be deduced. We were still supremely happy, but the manifestation of that happiness was changed: this was, in the first place, apparent from the character of our songs. In place of our "Row, Brothers, row," and "Merrily, merrily rung the Bells," which we had sported so gaily in the morning, our voices were engaged in singing, with great pathos, "Those Evening Bells," and such-like melancholy ditties. G——, in the mean time, was employed in parodying a passage from Parisina; and he had nearly dispelled the pathetic feelings induced by the "Evening Bells," from the laugh which it caused:—

> "The chapel bells are ringing
> Both mournfully and slow,
> In the grey round turret swinging,
> With a deep sound, to and fro;
> Heavily to the heart they go—
> Hark! the men are singing,
> For the bells, with notes of woe,
> They've often cursed for dunning so."

In the next place our regard was averted from ourselves and our boat, to the beauties of eve, and of the surrounding scenery.

It was one of those transcendent evenings, which, while from their very singularity at this time of the year, they appear more lovely, must necessarily send to the heart the feeling of summer. The sun was about setting behind the majestic walls of King's College Chapel (a fit resting-place for such a deity), and, ere he sank to repose, threw upon the waters a long line of liquid light, which,—

> " Unquenched, and glowing, appears to glide
> Like a lava-stream through the darker tide."

All nature was in harmony:—

> " There was not wind enough to twirl
> The one red leaf, the last of its clan,
> That dances as often as dance it can ;
> Hanging so light, and hanging so high,
> On the topmost twig that looks up at the sky."

And while, " in glorious sympathy with suns that set," we felt—

> " The softness of the hour
> Steal on the heart as dew along the flower,"

It is natural that our attention should also be directed to the objects which that sun now beautified.

The right bank of the river was fringed with its constant willows ; and on the left the undulating turf, the broken state of the ground, and the appearance of " ruined ruins" in the background, told that, in years past, this spot had been the residence of other beings ; but beings as quiet and innocent as the sheep which now fed there. This ground had formerly been the site of Barnwell Nunnery. In my usual manner, I felt very much inclined to moralize on the fate of the pale melancholy girls who once walked and prayed there. But, unfortunately for my sentimental ideas, I heard H— and B— in a violent dispute on a calculation of the odds against these same pale girls remaining nuns for one week, supposing the nunnery still to exist. They at last came to a conclusion; but the odds were so enormous, that I am afraid to venture on inserting them here; lest our mathematical talents should be questioned by some, who know not, so well as you or I, that in being—

"The first to scale a lady's bower,"

some Cambridge men would not yield to any Don Juan that ever existed.

But the sun shed his parting glory this evening on the heaving mound, as sweetly as ever he did in times of yore. And long may it be, before, on the spot where these gentle creatures lifted up their innocent faces to gaze on his departure, he shall smile on houses whose inhabitants, mocking the purity of a life they could not imitate, and laughing at the feelings they could not comprehend, will look equally upon his rise, meridian splendour, or decline,—

"Without the reverence and the rapture due
To that which keeps all earth from being as fragile
As I am in this form."

If you are not inclined to come the *Sir P. Teazle* part again, my boat-friends are. In my ecstasy, I unfortunately turned the rudder the wrong way, and made a sort of a tack—

"*Holloa, T——, what the devil are you at?*"—"*Oh! in the heroics.*"

"*Well, throw them off at present, or your long face may infect us,—and K—— begins to look pathetic.*"

" *Come, let's at least go in in style.*"

And this I believe we did : for, though I certainly perceived one or two gownsmen laughing, yet, to counter-
balance this, old Cross put on a most insinuating smile
and told us we " *kim in wall.*" *I* dare say he was righ-

The day, commenced in merriment, was concluded i-
noise, and if we any of us retired sober to bed, it wa-
not the fault of S——'s claret.——Well, adieu, I'm very tire-
of this long prosy letter, and if you are not the same, :
is only because you were long ago asleep. Believe m-
when you awake,

Your sincere and affectionate friend,

T——

Cambridge, March 6th, 1822.

LETTER II.

BREAKFAST-PARTIES.

DEAR SOUTH,—Differing so unfemininely, so mathematically, and so classically, from all other societies to which, in contra-distinction, the epithet of *worldly* may be applied, Cambridge and Oxford may well be considered as two rival and independent states—the Athens and Sparta of our northern clime.* The consequent dissimilarity of their manners and customs has often made it wonderful to me, that we can nowhere find any regular and familiar sketches of Cambridge or Oxford life. Unwilling to inquire whether want of interest might not be one of the causes which produced this, it followed immediately from this wonder that, partly for the sake of amusement to myself, partly from an idea that some small portion might be imparted to others,—I myself commenced a series of letters descriptive of the scenes in which I had been a participator; and of which I had been somewhat of a sentimental, somewhat of a philosophical, observer. I thought that the ladies' man might be curious to learn how we contrived to exist, when no

---

* I was lately reading an old MSS. book of Prophecies (or, rather, no prophecies, since I could have predicted as much), which wisely foretold, that this rivalry would cease, and one of the universities obtain an universally acknowledged superiority; when either Johnian puns should assume the complexion of Attic wit, or Oxford integrity, of Spartan probity—two events equally likely to happen.

longer basking in the life-inspiring beams of female beauty: flattering none, with none to reward our flattery; adoring none, with none to smile on our adoration: that the man of the world might wish to know what were the petty objects of our petty ambition, and the light amusements of our lighter hours; with few to own as masters, and little law to follow, but that of our own imaginations. I thought that the young and gay expectant of college pleasures might joy, while perusing my letters, in the anticipation of days to come; the mature inheritor of cares give a sigh for days gone by; and the gray-headed tenant of the elbow-chair, lamenting that,—

" Old times are changed, old manners gone,"

might relate the different scenes of *his* college life; and, exulting that there were happily no such doings in his time, might stamp his lamentations on the degeneracy of the rising generation, by the weight of reverence and authority which results from the awful shake of his old white hairs.

Such motives produced my last letter to you in the *Brighton;* but why they should not have been strong enough to elicit another, I cannot so well answer. Perhaps I was not pleased with my " Water-Parties;" perhaps it pleased not some others of my acquaintance; perhaps I saw in the writer of the " Long Vacation," one who, with an abler pen than mine, would save me the trouble of any farther concern about it. It is of little use adding any more perhapses, since they have all proved ineffectual against your remonstrances. And so, dear South, I send you my second letter.

You will perceive that, in the sentimental part of the

naracter I have assumed unto myself, I am still inclined
 look upon the innocent and blameless part of Cam-
ridge life ; and, while I can yet linger around the light,
m unwilling to throw up the darker shades.   I present
ιings exactly as they are, but take the liberty of choos-
ιg what the things shall be which I first present. Here-
fter, perhaps, when I come to write on other topics, it
ιay be wished that I had presented things as they are
ot—but of this anon.—

I continue, therefore, with a description of those par-
.es which all will equally allow should be disposed of at
ιe beginning of the day, but of which beginning itself
ll are not so well agreed ; some placing it at the actual
lawn, some a little later, and more at noon-day ;—
he gayer part of the community dating from the lat-
ιr, an hour before, or an hour after, according to the
ιarticular influence of sleep upon their eyes ; the read-
ιg part, and those to whom an imposition from the
lean, or a gratuitous lecture from the tutor, would be ra-
her inconvenient, maintaining the pre-eminence of the
ormer.   Though ranking myself distinctly under neither
ιead, I choose, at times, to assume all the agree-
bles of both ; and, finding a card on my table,

> " T——n, Trin. Coll.
>   " Breakfast.   Friday, 11 o'clock."   I hesitated
ιot to accept the invitation, although a breakfast-party,
ιxcept for the amusements of the day which sometimes
ollow it, is, in its regular Cambridge meaning, a " style
ιf thing which is my aversion."

Breakfast-parties are, indeed, of all others, the most
nsufferably stupid.   A company of men, some of whom
ιnow one another, perhaps ; some whose cups are ac-
ιuainted ; and others who have no more than seen one

another's face or gown; reading men and non-reading; mathematicians and fox-hunters; classics and coachmen; Olympic charioteers in theory, and four-in-hand whips in practice; crack *empty-bottles*, and full bottles cracked; shining stars and will-o'-the wisps: all may meet together in one common room, differing in opinions, manners, and tastes; and only agreeing in the one common point of eating. In this particular, indeed, there is no lack of entertainment: toast and muffins, ham and tongue, ducks and fowls, sausages and beefsteaks, red herrings and anchovies, pigeon pies and veal pies, snipes and wigeons, &c. &c., hot and cold, all vie with one another in most interesting and amiable profusion; and only yield in incongruity to the drinkables: chocolate, coffee, cocoa, tea, ale, porter, soda-water, and, in some instances, different sorts of wines*.

Such were the animate objects (fifteen in number, let be dogs, &c.), and such the inanimate (extending *ud n.*), which met my view on entering T——n's room, at half-

* To write this description for you alone would be something like sending coals to Newcastle; but I am in hopes that the sweet Brighton *belle*, as she sips her chocolate in bed, will deign to inquire how we manage these things at Cambridge.—Breakfast-parties, I must also tell her, are generally considered the most popular of our entertainments. The reading men patronize them because they take up least time; the non-reading men because they lead to other amusements; the Simeonite, because, from their very nature, they cannot be so objectionable as some others; the economist, because, being obliged to have some party, they are the least expensive. Some patronize them from convenience, others from choice, and others because they must have parties all day long.

past eleven, on the Friday.—(You remember T———n : just the same hearty blade as ever—by the by, what think you of T———n in love?—fact, 'pon honour !

"*Ah ! T———, old boy, how are you?*"

"*Here's a seat—chocolate or coffee?*" &c.

When those of the party whom I knew had asked me the usual number of questions, of how long I had been up, &c., and those whom I did not know, had given the usual inspection to my dress, appearance, &c., I was allowed to take my coffee and fowl in peace, and the general conversation, which my presence had for the moment interrupted, was resumed.

Horses and dogs, Newmarket and Melton hunt, stage-coaches and tandems, were severally, at the lower end of the table, the interesting topics of conversation.

P. then bet his horse for a race against Q.'s ; and Q. was astonished at his presumption. X. handed his plate for a snipe, and was ready to bet a wager he killed five snipes out of six. Y. laughed at X., and offered to go to the fens that very morning for a trial. An unfortunate Johnian made a pun ; but I could only hear the groans which followed it.

At the upper end of the table, occasionally interrupted by the vociferations of the lower, or by the pressing instances of our host to eat, the merits of the different colleges were discussed ;—the laxity of some—the discipline of others—the comparative strictness of lecturers or easiness of deans.

The conclusion seemed to be, that Trinity might do very well for those humdrums who patronized learning, but that, indisputably, Christ's was, in general, the sort of thing for a college. The mild and dignified urbanity of its master—the good fellowship of its fellows—the gay and gentlemanly character of the undergraduates—all received their due praise.

Apropos to masters, W——d begged pardon of the Trinitarians, but could not help d——g the whole race of " Milk and Waters." Hereupon, the Wordsworthians looked milk-and-watery.

Consequent to this ensued a discussion on poets, in which also some at the lower end joined.

B——e maintained that Percy Bysshe Shelley was utterly unintelligible : some thought differently; some thought it was very likely he might be; and some did not think at all.

J——f said that, for his part, he thought Barry Cornwall a devil of a good old chonck. Many seemed at fault; and one poor little gentleman, who had found some difficulty in learning what we were talking about, ventured to ask upon what branches of mathematics the last-mentioned gentleman had written, and whether Mr. J——f thought him equal to Whewell or Peacock ?

I, for my part, did just about the same as others, and talked as much sense or nonsense, which you please, as I conveniently could.

An awful pause in the whole conversation, soon after, indicated the conclusion of the first whet. This was at length broken, by an exclamation of S—r's—

" *C—k! you reprobate! where the devil were you last night—why came you not to my rooms, as agreed?*"

" *Could'nt find my way, i'faith—completely greased: never so drunk in my life. Dined with B—— of Trinity—eighteen bottles of claret among seven of us, let be Champagne. Set out for your rooms—found myself in bed this morning—clothes covered with mud—minus cap and gown—received a polite message from the proctor, that he should be happy to see me this morning, at half past ten. Told me he did me the honour to see me home last night—found me devil knows where: gave me two hundred lines of Homer to learn—hoped he would'nt think of such a thing: told him I could'nt learn them. All my eye—up to a trick —blow him!"*—

Here followed, of course, a general comparison of adventures with masters, tutors, deans, duns, snobs, &c. Some had been nabb'd at Barnwell, and some had given the proctor leg-bail; some had thrashed the bull-dogs, and some had bribed them. Some had got their heads broken by snobs, and some had broken snobs' heads. Some had written impositions, but not given them up, and some had given them up without having written them, &c. &c.

Again an attack was made upon the eatables, while the continual exclamations, " *Cursed good drink this!"*— " *Wholesome lap!"* &c., told, that the ale, porter, &c., were rapidly approaching to the evanescent state of vanishing fractions.

At length, the thoughts of Hall, and the reflection that it would be quite as well not to be seen drunk in the morning, seemed to have their due effects. The men lounged back upon their chairs or sofa; and a lazy sort of silence ensued, only broken by the occasional civilities of the breakfast-table.

" *What! aground? M——"*

" *You may say that,—regularly floor'd!"*

" *And you too, L——"*

" *Yes,—done up;—shall cut Hall to-day,—have had such a good blow-out here."*

When these sort of interjections had also ceased, and the men began to feel they must do something more than lounge upon the sofa all day, several amusements fo: the day were proposed, and, among the rest, a water-party

" *Talking of water-parties,*" says P., " *have you eve: seen a description of them in a magazine, called ' Th Brighton?' "*

Q. replied, that reading such things was quite out o his way.

X. said, that any one might have written as much.

Y. thought he himself could when he was at school ; but now, thank Heaven, it was a very different case ;—he did'nt come to Cambridge to write, and all that sort o thing.

M. spoke of the Brighton as altogether a cursed low style of thing,—but the poor wight had better have held his tongue, for he was immediately opened upon from all sides.

" *Pardon me, sir, but you cannot have given much attention to it,*" says I——f.

" *He's a Northite !*" whispers S——r.

" *He's a radical !*" says C——n.

" *He's a Johnian pig !*" says B——s.

" *The improvement since the first number is immense !*" says T——n.

" *You're right, old boy !*" says W——d.

And, although the ignorant wretch did not perhaps hear all this, yet he was cowed by plenty of black looks. The Brighton, therefore, upon the whole, came off with flying colours; and indeed one gentleman, who seemed to have his information from good sources, mysteriously hinted, that fear of your magazine was the cause of the long-expected Cambridge Quarterly's delay.

The water-party was arranged, and its members departed. Others, according to their reading humours, or

»ther various engagements, severally made their morning
:ongé, and vanished, till T——n, I——f, W——d,
B——s, S——r, and myself, were the only remaining
loiterers over the breakfast-table.

" *Who's a mind for a contemplative walk to the " Byro-
nian Grove ?* "

S——r. " *Where the devil is that ?*"

I——f. " *What ! you a third-year man, S——r, and
not know Lord Byron's walk? Out upon you! Come,
then, place yourself under our guidance, and you shall not
repent it. Wordsworthian as you are, you shall own it as
a spot that Wordsworth himself, in his most fastidious
moods, might have selected for meditation.*"

W——d. " *You're right, old boy !*"

To Lord Byron's walk, therefore, as nothing better
was proposed, we resolved to adjourn. We mounted our
caps and gowns—passed by the back of Queen's Coll.,
and were soon in full progress over the fields to Granchester.

It was sufficient for happiness that there was a clear
blue sky above us, and that the pure healthy breeze of
an April morn floated around us—but the very nature
of a walk forcing too strongly upon us an idea of the
constitutional walks of reading men, forbade this happiness to be more than tranquil, while our conversation
and amusement by the way was of that character which
is so felicitously described in one of the introductory
epistles to Marmion :—

> " To thee, perchance, this rambling strain
>   Recals our summer walks again,
> When, doing nought, and, to speak true,
> Not anxious to find ought to do,

The wild unbounded hills we rang'd ;
While oft our talk its topic chang'd.
And, variable as our way,
Rang'd unconfin'd from grave to gay.
——————————— full oft we could pursue
Our walk in social silence too."

The country round Cambridge has been frequently
depicted as totally devoid of attraction : and it is not
difficult to conjecture the causes of such a misrepresentation. Cambridge men are not in general much ad-
dicted to a search after the picturesque, and are moreover predisposed to imagine this search would be ineffectual, from the notions of flatness and barrenness
which have been imprinted on their minds while pursuing their sports of hunting and shooting over the open
country. Others are too much absorbed in mathematical reveries to do more than now and then raise their
eyes to calculate the particular distance of some particular object ; and the greater number are well contented
to see with other people's eyes, and to say just what
they hear said by others. That it is a misrepresentation,
however, you are fully aware ; and let the sweet Brighton beauty be willing, till she can visit Cambridge, to
see with my eyes ; and when I shall be at Brighton, I
will readily promise that the light of her's shall colour
all my objects. Let her accompany us in our walk, to
where an extended green, sloping gradually to the Cam,
and bounded on the flank by a rural hamlet, indicates
the vicinity of the village of Granchester. Here let her
pause, and, turning in the direction of the Cam, which
rolls below at the distance of about 150 paces, she will
see, " I ween, a full fair sight." Directing the eye

across the wide meadow which lies between the Cam and the village of Trumpington, the first object which attracts the attention is the white castellated turret of Trumpington Church, rising, at the distance of about one quarter of a mile, in solemn sublimity, above the condensed mass of clustering elms; like a good and great man, retiring from the noise and pomp of the world to make his vassals happy,—so happy do trees appear, as they wave in the spring breeze, to that holy church. A little farther to the left, the density of the elms is again broken, to give a view of the old manor-house of Trumpington; which, by its adjacency to the church, may be supposed to present the idea of the good steward who has grown gray and respected in the service of that good and great master.

The whole front of these elms is breasted by a fringe of firs and beeches, &c., whose elegant and waving shapes, and light green verdure, make a fine contrast with the dignified family solemnity of the elms; and, at this distance, present the same sort of appearance as that which is sometimes afforded by a field, partially il-lumined by the rays of a partially clouded sun, while the rest is left in shade.

It is by this same species of larch, firs, &c., stretch-ing away towards the left, that the horizon, in the dis-tance, is bounded. They skirt the whole length of the Trumpington road; and the shapes into which their co-nical tops seem, at this point of view, to cut the ho-rizon, are the vandykes which are sometimes seen to form the flounce or other ornament of a lady's dress: though, I must own that, in the case of these said van-dykes waving round a neat ankle, 'or serving to reveal "short glimpses of a breast of snow," few of us Cantabs would have stood meditating with such fearless confidence, and calm equanimity, as that with which we now gazed on the light green firs, and the clear blue sky.

In the valley below, gliding away like happiness, and "making its waves a blessing as they flow," the quiet Cam quietly pursued its serpentine course. While the leafy road which connected Trumpington with Granchester, the mill on that road, and the Granchester church of elegiacal celebrity, completed on the right a felicitous picture, such as is not often met with; and such as, sweet lady, you could not show me at Brighton. You will tell me, perhaps, to stand on the downs, and look at the "wide wide sea." But I will answer that the sight of the eternal ocean only forces upon me too abruptly an idea of my own insignificance, to allow me to indulge anything but awe: that "my spirit is mute in the presence of power:" that by the sea-shore I am lost—but that here, here, in this quiet scene, "I feel indeed I am a man," with all his love, powers, and sweet imaginations. You are not satisfied yet, perhaps: your mind has been attuned to something grander. Well— we can meet you even here. Turn directly round upon Cambridge, and the view of King's College Chapel, towering in unapproachable grandeur above the diminished colleges, will almost impress you with an idea that you ought to have been blind to aught else, and will inspire you with many of those feelings which have been made familiar to you on your native shore.

It is a sight which must have its due, though various effects, upon all. Many would own the imperious necessity of bursting forth in its praise; and more the obligation of feeling its beauty in silence. The silence

o

however, of the tongue is temporary; and the feeling of the heart may endure till heart and tongue are alike at rest in the grave. It is from this cause, perhaps, that, familiar as King's College Chapel had become to us, we were still inclined to regard it with all the feeling, but not with all the silence, of early acquaintainceship. Much was said that I have no doubt was often said before, with much the same emotion. If each of us had been alone, this would certainly have endured to the point of sending us away moralizing and melancholy: but the circumstance of our being in company, and the necessity which every one felt of not being behind-hand in saying something extraordinary for the amusement of the rest, greatly tended to impair the delicacy of our feeling. No question will be made of this, when I mention some of the comparisons which our emulation produced :—

T———n ("magna componere parvis") compared the appearance of the chapel to that of a hog on a moor, in a high wind, with all its bristles erect, and all its pigs around it. And this comparison ought to be borne in mind by all those who wish to have any light thrown before Byron's controversy with Bowles.

I———f compared its appearance, at this distance, to the idea which had been left upon his mind, by what he had somewhere read of the great sea-serpent, rearing its immense length of neck from the waters, and calmly gazing around, without deigning to notice the sensation its presence had caused.

B———s, to that of Robinson Crusoe's ship amid the canoes of the savages.

W———d, to that of an oblong bed of tulips in a garden of cabbages ; or a banyan-tree in a field of tobacco.

S————r, to Lord Byron among the poets.

" *You might just as well have said, S————r to a proctor among the bull-dogs! Why, my dear fellow, what the devil has Lord Byron to do with a chapel?—Cambridge with poetry?—or Cambridge men with poets? S————r! S————r! you will never be a wrangler! but there might still be some hope for you, if Lord Byron should ever have any influence on a mathematical pate!*"

Comparisons may be ludicrous without throwing a shade of contempt upon the superior object of the comparison ; it is to the inferior, and consequently, in this case, to almost all nature, that the odium would be attached. Our reverence therefore was not diminished because we had laughed, although it certainly was not of that sublime species which the poor pagan, in his ignorance, would have felt; who, turning round to gaze on this structure, would have bowed down, exclaiming " Behold the God who created all this beauty." We might envy the intensity of the feeling itself, but not the primary ideas which produced it.

And you, fair lady, imaginary companion of our way ! you would say, with the aptest comparison, that the view of this chapel reminded you of the broadside of the men-of-war you have sometimes seen off Brighton, while all their sails are set, and they are about to bear to distant lands the learning and produce of a happier clime, with the knowledge of the God who made it happier. And I should compare it—to what ?—to your own sweet self,—

> " When, 'mid your handmaids in the hall,
> You stand superior to them all."

Go then,—return to your own dear sea; but, when you wander on its shore, let the memory of a scene that lives but in mental review mix with the pleasureable impulses of the present. Go—walk on the Steyne, and tell your friends with what canny youths you have spent the morning—gaze on the splendid mansion of the great king of a great people, and tell them that you have looked on the more splendid residence of a greater sovereign—describe it to them in all its beauty—and, if an idea of the tenth part only of its sublimity be imparted, then not in vain, dear lady, shall we have walked together.

But stay, lady! linger yet a little while on this spot, and you may trace our route to yon farther bridge, that passes over a branch of the Cam. To the eye it is but an arrow-flight, and the lineaments of those two gownsmen who are talking there are almost distinguishable. But swift feet cannot travel so fast as bright eyes, and our's cannot be very swift in leaving you. Our path, moreover, is circular, and we must travel it, with but the tantalizing idea of how pleasant it wou'd be to see its beauty reflected on fair faces. Now we pass by Granchester Church; now you catch a glimpse of us crossing the meadow in which you see that neat cottage; now winding round the brier-decked pathway which leads to the mill; the mill is passed; and once more, for the last time, a parting glance of us is obtained at the destined bridge. One wave of the hand, and so farewell:—

> " By church, by mill, by hawthorn-tree,
>   Each after each are disappearing;
>   Each after each, their tassels rearing,
>   Upon the farther bridge you see."

And now, I fear, I must bid *you* farewell. The matter of my proposed subjects has increased so much, in its progress, beyond my previous intention, that I am obliged to pauze for the present, in order to keep within the limits of a letter. Before I could possibly give you a saunter in Lord Byron's walk, and re-conduct you to Cambridge by Pemberton's, your patience and mine will be pretty well agreed in taking leave of us.

Ever your's sincerely,

T——.

LETTER III.

THE LONG VACATION,

BEING A TRUE AND FAITHFUL ACCOUNT OF THE PIL-
GRIMAGE OF A "JESUIT" TO THE BANKS
OF CAM, IN THE DOG-DAYS.

MANY days and months have passed away into the
mists of time, since you and I, dear South, enjoyed together the luxuries and the seclusion of a college life ;
since we rambled, arm-in-arm, in the sacred walks of
Trinity, lingered in rapture beneath the air-hung dome
of King's, or coasted the stagnant waters of that noted
stream which guards the groves of Jesus, in our passage
to the sluices ; since we hurried forth, from the distrac-
tions of the schools or the lecture-room, to look after country prospects and country damsels, upon the narrow pathway that leads to Granchester; since we made our pilgrimage to the ennobled, though humble church of Madingley,
where Gray is said to have composed that most exquisite of
English elegies, the " Elegy in a Country Church-yard ;"
since we trimmed our little sail upon the Cam ; since
we studied the *angles* and *cannons* of mine host of the
Three Tuns at Chesterton, in preference to the *angles* of
Dominus Euclid, or the *canons* of Porson ; since we
wooed the invigorating breezes upon the hills of Gog
and Magog till we had forgotten the balmy *airs* of He-
licon ; since we deemed all that was respectable or
learned was hid beneath a " curtain " of prince's stuff,
or a tassel of black silk ; since, in short, the name of

" gownsman " was our delight, and the name of "snob" our curse.

Our examinations are now all over; our fees all paid; our terms all completed ; our studies finished; and our success determined ; and we may now go forth from the land of gowns to the land of petticoats, and prove, if we please, that there may be a parodox in nature as well as in ecclesiastical lore, by exhibiting ourselves as *married bachelors.*

We can now look upon the inconveniences of an university life with a smile, and on its gratifications with a sense of past delight : the name of lecturer, or tutor, or dean, or master, or proctor, or vice-chancellor, pass away unheeded ; and we have long ceased to shudder at the sight of a moderator's man.

Yet, methinks, you have not altogether so bent your mind upon the affairs of this busy world, as to be indifferent to the good or evil report, the increasing or decreasing fame of that place which your youthful labours rendered dear, or your youthful frolics rendered memorable ;—of those scenes, which beheld, and protected, and encouraged, and rewarded, the exertions of your " literary hours."

As to myself, I do confess, I have still a yearning after old sports and pastimes, old studies and pursuits ; and, though in rural retirement and learned leisure, surrounded by all the charms of a beautiful country and a happy fire-side, I never hear the sound of college or hall, but my heart leaps up again, and I am, in imagination, transported once more into the magic land of signs and symbols, and enshrined in the venerable buildings and classic aisles of our good old Alma Mater.'

Perhaps, however, your fate hath never been to visit Granta, when the suns and the silence of autumn have proclaimed universal and university holidays; when the bustle of a short term hath yielded to the inactivity of a long vacation; when the wisdom and *wiggerism* of Golgotha have disappeared, and the organ of St. Mary's hath pealed "its choral strains" to an almost empty *pit*, and still emptier *galleries;* when cloisters and courts are alike silent in their desolation, and the combination-room hath left its revel and gaiety to the porter's lodge and servant's hall.

That there is such a time last August afforded me a proof; and, as the thousand mathematical eyes who, in the fury of friendship and joy, at sight of the Brighton Magazine (and I will say, Cambridge Magazine), will yet bear recollection of the concise demonstration and proof positive of Newton and Eudoxus, I will even bring to my mind the observation of the late venerable Professor Vince, that a theorem without a proof, like a coat without sleeves, is worth naught; and, in the true spirit of scholastic consequence, demonstrate as clearly as I can, that "Cambridge, in the long vacation, is, like Mr. Trevelyan's essay on Puns, very dull and stupid."

I had not been in Cambridge for many months;—the last time I resided there, was during the full bustle of an October term, when Freshmen looking stupid things, Sophs looking wicked things, and questionists wise things, met me at every step, and gowns of every cut and colour which the skill of the schneider or fancy of the dyer could invent, formed such an impenetrable phalanx of stuff and silks, that one might have fancied the times back " when all wore gowns," and, as Tacitus

says, " the sexes were scarcely distinguishable." As I
threw myself from the coach-box, I exclaimed, in all the
warmth of filial affection, like Wolsey at the gate of
Leicester Abbey,—" I am come," once more, " to lay
my bones amongst you," ye venerable spires and ancient
domes! It is a joyous moment, when we return to the
dearly-cherished scenes of our youth, at an unexpected
time; and thus it was with me. The vehicle, under the
able conduct of John Smith, landed me safely at the office of that well-known sign (scarcely less noted than
its predecessor of the tusk, in merry East-Cheap,) the
Cerulean Pig of the Cantabs; and, as soon as I had
tipped the coachee, and parcelled off my luggage for
the "gentleman in waiting," and given directions respecting it to the *sour-visaged* landlady, I sallied forth
to seek a domicile, as my intention was to stay a week
or more.

As I paced along the pavement, I felt a sensation
for which I could not account,—it was that of loneliness ;
and yet how could I be lonely amidst the remembrances
of gleesome days of "auld lang syne?"—I entered
Deighton's shop; but it was unfrequented : the books
stood in undisturbed security on the shelves, and the
counters showed no marks of the prying haste which
discomposes many volumes in the search for one, and
which sometimes is rather a nuisance to the order-lov-
ing shopman, who stands sulkily by, whilst the book-
worm, scorning knife or ivory, applies his, perhaps,
unwashed fingers in the separation of hot-pressed fine-
wove duodecimos. There appeared to be nothing new,
because of purchasers there were not many ; and the
only volumes which revelled in all the purity of their
pristine whiteness, and free from tossings from one

learned hand to another, which the others had been blessed with, were the ponderous tomes of the French mathematicians, or the perhaps smaller, though certainly not less expensive and less useful ones, of our Englsih analyst, Professor W——, and his mechanical friend the Dean of E——.

There was no one within, so I once more started on my travels. "Whither shall I go?" said I to myself, as I stood upon the lower step of the door-way. "To St. Rhadegund's," whispered my conscience; for I felt persuaded I ought to pay my devoirs at her shrine first. "About ship," said I to myself: and I accordingly took my way towards that best-beloved of all university attractions. I could not be but struck with the silence and solemnity which reigned in undisputed sway over the streets through which I wandered; and, as I cast a glance towards the venerable gateway of that learned pile, where Newton had pondered, and Barrow had studied, I thought of the hundreds I had seen on some saint's day, or its eve, arrayed in vestal white, crowding from evening chapel. All-Saint's church-yard seemed all gloom: and Sidney Street, that field of many a fray and feud, that territory of the whiskered king, seemed as still as if the name of "gownsman" had never echoed in it; the poplars waved to and fro with a sort of melancholy motion, over the heavy red-brick walls, and, save the insects, which flitted amongst their leaves, were the only representatives of motion in the street, from Magdalen Bridge to Trinity Church: not a coach; not a bargee; not even he of the "three-nuikt hat" and the quiz-glass,—the notorious Jemmy Gordon. I hastened down, almost involuntarily, the narrow serpentine lane, which in religious times was looked upon with a degree of sacredness, as its

name implies ; not a footstep, save mine own, paced along
the pavement; and I thought that, had Mr. Maberley (the
Joseph of Cambridge, and the Vitruvius of Chesterton)
ever seen it so still, he might have been spared the mor-
tification of seeing his edifying pamphlet on the corrup-
tions of that street, divested of its hypocrisy. I thought
of the changes and the chances of the Freshman's life,
from the time of his coming up from boarding-school, a
raw and inexperienced *spooney*, to the time of his going
down again,—less liable to insult, but more liable to
laughter,—the knight of the *spoon;* and whilst I thought
thereon I sighed ;—but not for myself. I had a friend
who thus went off with triumphing in his disappoint-
ment, proud and pleased, through very spite of himself,
at his mighty honour, like the sun from the clouds of
November, smiling amidst gloom : but, alas ! his joy
was short, and the stigma attached unjustly to that man
who happens to have a name best suited for the occasion
of the ridiculous epithet, caused such depression of spirits and consequent loss of health, that the church-yard
shortly received him fresh from the senate-house, amidst
the countless multitudes who had, unhonoured, yet
more honoured, staid their time on earth, ere called
away. Surely the planners of our university laws have
somewhat to answer for, in thus allowing their favours
to bring disgrace upon, perhaps, their worthiest members ; and, whilst the name of Senior Wrangler and the
gradations of Senior Optimis bring respect—whilst
they have golden and silver spoons in abundance,—why
add to their store of distinguishments the paltry wooden
one,—that which causes more disgrace to attach to individuals, colleges, and examiners, than all the bene-
fits derived from the institutions of their benefactors

can do away with? Oxford proceeds on a better plan;
and, contented, if it cannot speak in praise, to be silent,
in a happy measure mingles all in one common lot.
Why, when the sister university has set the example,
and her precedent has been followed in nearly the most
trivial circumstances, will the hand of power refrain from
blotting out the decree from its rolls, which thus stigma-
tizes all, from the highest to the lowest?

Behold me, then, once-more, at the gate-way of the
" ever-honoured Jesus," as Mr. Coleridge, himself a
Jesuit, has excellently said. The trees which overhang
the lofty wall on each side shed a melancholy gloom
over the road, and darkened the almost untenanted " bar-
racks." The long avenue was still; not a step was
heard, nor a voice came from the inner courts; the windows in the long front were all blinded; and the very
weeds, which are so beautiful an ornament to the walls
on either side (and which a barbarous taste would, a
year or two ago, have rooted up), seemed rioting in desolation. The hands on the chapel-dial pointed to the
hour of six, the well-known hour when I have listened
with pleasure to the heavy peal of the solitary bell,
which told the time of—

" Prayers, and thanks, and bended knees;"

And, as the numbered tones fell upon my ear, memory,
for the moment, aroused the dearest associations which
connected me with the walls I was gazing on, and these
gave place to feelings of a more agonizing nature. Still-
ness was over all, as of a canopy. No rustling of gowns;
no hurrying of *time-saving* worshippers (frequenters of
chapel not for the love of God, but the dread of the

dean); no passing salutations, as acquaintances met,
betrayed the character of the place I then stood
in. I half doubted whether I ought to proceed,
—" Shall I not," said I, inwardly, " be an intruder
on this solitude?—but, no! these gates will never forbid *my* entrance;" and I hastened forward. The
porter's lodge was barred. The gate was open—and I
entered the first of our three small, though neat quadrangles. An air of unusual gloom was here also; the
grass had attained an enormous length for the time of
year, and plainly showed that neither scythe nor foot had
lately touched it: there was a time, when I had strayed
over it, in spite and defiance of the herb-loving fellows,
merely to show that I did not regard their whims a
blade of grass; but I could not then, and I would not
have intruded upon the sacred plot for all the hay in
Christendom. I was doubtful whether to return or ex-
plore yet further; when the figure of chanticleer, over the
entrance to the cloisters, invited me to wander there.
As I passed along, the awful silence and darkness of the
place again awoke me to remembrance of long-past days,
and I thought on " Auld-lang-syne," till every action of
my college life rose before me like the spirits of the
murdered to Macbeth. It was in this part of the college
that I had *kept* the better part of my time. I ascended
the stairs leading to my old apartments. The door, as
we were wont to say, was *sported*, yet bearing, upon its
rough coat of black, the impressions of my friend
W——'s knuckles. The sight recalled his image to my
mind, and I bethought me of his merry-looking face,—
his neat gentleman-like appearance; and, withal, that
fund of inexhaustible humour which sparkled in his eye.
I bethought me of days long gone, when he and I had,

in the warmth of feeling, and hey-day of youth, strolled forth from that very door-way, for our noon-tide saunter or evening voyage : I thought of that witching time of night, when, after taking our " pint-stoup" of negus or our beaker of milk-punch, we had gone forth " like the Chaldeans to watch the stars ;" or, like Brutus his dog, to " bay the moon*," or rather like the university wakes, as they may justly be called, to serenade the fellows with " song, and harp, and minstrel lore." " Days of my youth," thought I, with the Honourable Mr. ——, of Virginia, " ye are vanished away." Time has passed heavily with me since these walls echoed to *my* ears the merry laugh or still merrier chorus? " As I mused thereon," a sound came from the opposite side of the court ; was it, thought I, from those rooms where the other worthy member of our triumvirate has joined us so often in the praise of wine and song?—but he too was away ; and the sound which I heard was the dull shriek of a starling from the chapel-tower. As I was about to retire, the entrance to the hall met my vision ; how could I pass unnoticed the scene of our feastings and our examination? I scrambled up the steps, and again stood beneath the roof where I had so often stood before ; the heavy cloth-covered door creaked on its hinges with a dull and monotonous sound, and then shut with a clap which plainly told it closed upon a solitude. All was quiet here, the tables shining from their unstained varnish, and the venerable features of Tobias Rustat and the Archbishops Sterne and Cranmer, in the same position as when I last gazed on them ; " it is," said I, with the motto above them, " *semper eadem.*" But there was an air of gloom in their house

* Shakspeare, Jul. Cæs. Act IV. the *Tent-Scene.*

of feasting. The very portraits on the dark walls seemed anxiously looking for the wonted banquet. " And was it here that I have often tasted puddings à la college and charlotte worthy the palate of a Lucullus, and cracked puns worthy the ears of a Johnian? Was it here," said I, " that I have plied the *graceless* knife and graceful joke? Was it here I fagged at $+$ and $-$, x and y, till I almost forgot my a, b, c? Was it here I *funked* at Mr. ——'s *plain and literal translations?*" and, in order to save a place " *above the mark,*" as the Oxonians say, that I murdered chronology as easily as Napoleon did his janissaries; that I metamorphosed logarithms and differences so much like my predecessor of *the nose,* good master Ovid, that I, at last, found the difference between philosophy and common sense to be a maximum in my case, and discovered my head to be a log, and that Lacroix's book, like that of the associate *calculists,* was all d——d stuff? " Was it here"——I was proceeding, like a hero of the buskin, in my soliloquy, when my lucubrations were prevented by the entrance from the combination-room, of, as I thought, one of the fellows. " Well," said I, " my Jesuit, thy house is *not* left unto thee desolate!" The person who entered bore all the appearance, by his dress, of a gentleman; and, imagining he might be a friend, I accordingly doffed my beaver and bared my fist for a salute; but, ye gods! what did I see, why my own *gyp,* dandified to a degree of wonderment, his collar starched stiff as buckram, his *cloth* as knowing as any fellow-commoner's, or London apprentice's on a Sunday,—his coat of the newest fashion, and his legs— O ye sons of Crispin, like those of whom Homer has sung,—the ευκνημιδες Αχαιοι, well booted and spurred Said I, after a gaze of some minutes, astonished and half mad at the fellow's foolery, " Why ———, what the deuce has become of you all ? fellows, fellow-commoners, pensioners, and all gone and vanished away, as if such had never been! I have rambled through courts, cloisters, and hall; and at last have discovered, that there is yet an inhabitant in these walls, though like the bottle whose wine is gone and filled with air. Now all the wit and wisdom and power is departed, fools and asses fill their places: where are they all?" The maulkin answered with a congé, as low as his laundress's labour would allow him, " 'Tis the long vacation, sir; and you know, sir, our masters are all gone down, and"—and, rejoined I, impatiently, " left their servants to keep up the appearance of stupidity and absurdity, by presenting themselves as living caricatures of *their* puppyism and folly! But where is the master?"—" In town, sir."—" The dean?"—" At Cheltenham, sir."—" The tutor?"—" On the continent, sir."—" And so, said I, as soon as I could collect the true account of their absence, " the tutor is ' pricking' over the Apennines, on a broken-kneed mule, or tracking the path of Hannibal over the Alps, or scribbling bad Greek and radicalism in a monkish album, in imitation of my Lord Byron, or some other curiosity of the day, or, perhaps, scratching the symbolic representations of $\square$ $\triangle$ or $\sqrt{}$, or any other *a b surd* idea, upon the glaciers of Mont St. Bernard, and chuckling over the fancy that some future traveller will put them down in his note-book, as proofs that the ice has existed before the flood, and that these are the remains of some præ-Adamitic inscription; and, as if this were not enough, the dean is, I suppose, squandering his health, his manners, and his chapel-fines, at a watering-place; and the master gone preferment-hunting to Carlton House; and these ancient and religious foundations left to jackdaws and jackasses and jackanapes! Shades of Alcock and Cranmer, look not down in wrath upon the walls ye did adorn and build, but rather in pity and forgiveness; the tide will soon return and bear the weeds which now sail so gaily down the channel to their own native ooze, and all will again be right." As I spake this, I left the hall and the *gyp*, the latter wondering whether his old master had taken a lease of the witlings of Bedlam, or whether his senses had taken leave of him. I was sorry afterwards that I had spoken so severely of those good friends of order and preservers of old institutions, the officers of the place; for I have often had reason to speak well of their kindness and attention, which, notwithstanding the momentary forgetfulness of them which my "man of men" occasioned, I can never wholly eradicate from my mind. Peace be with them, and my humble benison! Their lot is not the most agreeable, and though, perhaps, they enjoy the "*otium cum dignitate*," yet they often feel the reversed lot of "single *blessedness*." I now walked out towards the grove, passed the closed doors of buttery and kitchen, those storehouses of punch and beef-steaks, where I had often issued orders for a nightly frolic or Sunday-morning festival. You must remember the little court with its narrow sward and lilac trees, and the traceries of the hall-window, jutting from amidst the ivy which creeps up the old wall of the college, and the iron gateway at the end, and the green fields peeping through the interstices of the rails, and the distant flow of the river, all affording a pleasing and not unenviable change to the darkness and obscurity of cloisters and corridors And I have reason to remember it too. Often have I scaled those walls and that gate, at the hazard of my neck

and my terms, to save a sixpenny fine, or escape a twen-
ty-line imposition for keeping late hours; and often have
I sat like " Niobe, all tears," in a dead *funk* at top of that
little building in the corner, when a solitary step approaching has alarmed me in my fancied cunningness,
lest I should be discovered.   Oh, I never shall forget the
time when a tile which my careless foot had loosened,
fell before a poor Freshman, who was musing in careless
loneliness at the murky midnight of one December Sa-
turday; away he scampered, believing that St. Rhadegund, or some of her nuns, had come out to accompany
him in his dreams of imagination: poor wretch! I believe
he was planning a poem upon evening, and had come
out for poetical ideas upon the subject.   The report next
morning was, that the college was haunted, and that the
said Freshman poet and poetical Freshman, in the fury of
inspiration, " his eye rolling in a fine frenzy," to the
roof of ——, actually saw the spirit of old *Alcock*, in a
flannel dressing-gown and red nightcap, in a posture of
humiliation, looking like Marius over the ruins of Car-
thage, upon the walls he had founded.   And, to tell the
truth, I was glad it was credited; for it was generally understood that I personated the worthy bishop that evening; in my hurry I having dropped the cap which I borrowed of a friend (my own being lost in a " row" with the
bargees.)   This cap was known by its owner's private
mark, " Golgotha," and, as it was brought to me next
morning, I said, " Golgotha! rightly art thou named,
for the place of a skull thou art, and a precious *numskull*
too!   This and many other scenes of *knight-errantry* came
fresh to my memory, and, as I sauntered up the walk,
" I fought all my old battles o'er again," and lived again
n all the fancied pleasures and freaks of college term-

keeping. But, alas! how changed was this place, sinc
I last walked in it, in the pride of cap and gown. Th
grass was growing between the flints which paved th
narrow pathway, and the sparrows alone proved that li
was not wholly gone. I reached the gate, and on th
brick pillar which forms one support for it, I gazed invo
luntarily ; for it had often pleasured me to look upon
name which, cut there, had rendered it immortal: th
name, yet remaining, was that of *Gilbert Wakefield*,
name ever dear to the scholar or the man of feeling; ar
can you wonder, as a Jesuit, I should have recognise
the characters with acuteness of enjoyment? Perhap
in a moment of ennui—perhaps when a Freshman, it w
sculptured there, little thinking that he should thereaft
raise, by his own industry and from his brain, a mon
ment far more lasting,—far more pleasing, than pillars
brick and stone. Fame has immortalized him, and I
might have left to his *gyp* the short-lived reputatic
which a piece of Sheffield cutlery has here betrayed
have been his desire. He may say, indeed, wi
Horace,—

> " Exegi monumentum ære perennius
> Regalique situ pyramidum altius ?"

I took a parting glance, and, returning through the shad
of the cloisters and courts, again found myself at the e
terior gateway of the college.

It was now approaching towards sunset : the eveni
was beautifully mild, the sky of a deep blue, set off
some light clouds, which partly shone in their native p
rity, and partly glittered in the farewell beams of the d
scending luminary. The west was one blush of crimso
the town was silent and dark, save where the many-

gured spires and turrets of the college gates and chapels smiled in the last blaze of splendour. I sauntered off to enjoy the mildness of the season, upon the "pieces" which separate, though serving to connect, the respective mansions of our academical residence.

But I here found that the town was yet alive;—the road from Barnwell was literally crowded and covered with the families of the townsfolk returning from their evening walk. I recognised many *gyps* and college servants amongst them, all aping, by their demeanour, the manners of their betters, and elocutionizing, in strains of Ciceronian volubility, upon subjects of every kind, whether calculated or not for the abilities of the speaker to express, or the mind of the hearer to comprehend. There appeared the same studied kind of false gentility amongst the tradespeople; and I could not help being amused as the successive parties passed me, at the ideas presented to me by this motley group of borrowed manners, and perhaps I should not be wrong to say, *stolen* consequence.

The men endeavoured to look honest, and the women, I could observe, wished to be thought modest. As I was hastening from them, and about to turn down towards Emmanuel, I was accosted by the only gownsman I had yet seen, my old friend N——. A mutual start of surprise was followed by mutual congratulations and mutual inquiries, and the conference ended by our joining company, and adjourning to his quarters. As soon as I could get an opportunity of asking him a few questions, unconnected with the immediate cause of our satisfaction at meeting thus unexpectedly, I stated to him my disgust at finding Cambridge so much altered from what I *had* known it. " I have been," said I, " to the north, rambling amidst mountains, and lakes, and waterfalls.

and drinking in the inspiration of song and quietude, from the most beautiful scenes of nature, and am now, on my return to my friends, refreshed and delighted with my tour. I thought, however, to have derived some gratification by taking this good old place in my way, not doubting that I should have met with, at least, some old faces and old friends; but I am horribly disappointed, and, after having come with the determination to stay a week or two, I find myself, after a few hours' residence, re-determined to do no such thing. I shall instantly away, and leave my promised stay to some future time, when loneliness will not alone reign predominant." —" You are right," said he, " you are right ; and, when we have discussed a few cups of that beverage of which it has been said,—

' Nec tecum vivere possum, nec sine *te*,'

I will give a few plain and positive reasons for the propriety of such a measure." We had by this time reached the walks of Trinity, now untenanted, except where a few bed-makers were studying attitudes on the brink of the river: and, in a few minutes, were once more within the sound of *gyp-room* and *sizings*. We quaffed our chalked milk and water quietly enough, and passed a pleasant evening very *agreeably*, as the cockney has it and, though our conversation was not so edifying as one might imagine it would have been, had *the bard of Ri mini* and his friend " *Jupiter*," and that " *magnum Jovi incrementum*," the late (or as R—, of St. John's, would say, the " defunkit") Johnny Keats, been present; yet on the whole, it was " mighty good, truly." After *bitc* had been removed (we request our female readers not to

be alarmed—the Gradus ad Cantab, a work eminently
useful, when reading of Cantabs and their amusements,
will satisfy their scruples), N—— addressed me " as follows" (so saith the reporter of the radical meetings in this
part of the world); but as I had forgotten to bring my
scribe with me, and I cannot write *short*-hand (as may
be evidenced by the length of this article, which I crave
pardon for, of your thousands of readers), I will not take
upon me to say I report verbatim; nevertheless, the observations my friend made will serve to show that my original theorem (for I must regard the Euclidizing Freshman), was not without proof. " I have been," said he,
" a constant resident in the university, term and non-
term, since the beginning of last October, and have, of
course, seen Cambridge in all the gaiety which the return
of the *men* never fails to bring, and in all the dulness
which their *going down* always produces. I have resided
here through the greater part of four successive years,
and have enjoyed the idleness of a college life, as well as
bowed my back beneath the weight of college discipline;
and I do assure you, candidly, that I would rather be
subjected to the *bore* of lectures, schools, and senate-
house, for twenty years to come, than have the task of residing again through ' the long vacation.' We rise late
or early, as we please; no sound of the matin-bell to
awake us to devotion and mathematics, no vesper-bell to
call us away from wine and wit, to pray out our ' *times*,'
no dread of being ' put out of sizings and commons,' at
et the whim or the caprice of a ' senior,' or ' dean,' to
disturb our serenity of mind. But these blessings, *if
such they may be called*, are amply compensated by a
' number numberless' of contrary circumstances. The
few who stay here during the summer are put to sad

shifts to amuse themselves, when tired with reading
there are no morning calls to be made or received; n
invitations ' to wine' to be given or rejected; no plan
to be laid for the next morn's ramble. One cannot al
ways be 'at work;' and to fly to a newspaper for re
laxation, and puzzle the brain with politics, after si
hours' hard fag at Thucydides or Newton, is no sinecure
particularly as the speculations of modern writers are al
most as intelligible, and certainly as unedifying, as th
' riddle of the Sphinx,' *therefore*, as we say in argu
ment, the *Union* is but little looked to in the summer.
sometimes feel inclined to play a rubber at billiards, bu
there is no one to play with; and if I would try my hand
at a cricket-bat, the ground is covered with none bu
' snobs;'—so, from day to day I linger on, amids
books and papers, sickened and unsatisfied, like th
starling which Sterne tells of, always exclaiming,—' :
can't get out :' for, if I would, there is a drawback or
my scheme, and I must suffer other hands than my own
to gather the fruit in my own garden; other arms to sup
port the slender forms of those who would fly to *me* for
protection ; other eyes to behold, and other ears to listen
to, the sweet, fond, and kind speeches of my fair friends
at home ; whilst, with the dread of an examination, and
the fear of a failure, I am still at college, alone and un-
happy, waiting the decision of a vacant fellowship;
which, if attained, will scarcely recompense me for the
trouble and uneasiness it has occasioned me. But this is
not all : the catalogue of long-vacation miseries is an almost endless one, and any one who understands calculation might show it could be extended ' *ad infinitum*,' as
easily as Dr. Wood proves the *infinite divisibility* of a
piece of mahogany. The comforts of a college room,

which, at other times, amply compensate the nuisance of term-keeping, are, in some measure, denied to us; our *gyps* are grown so saucy and so smart, such puppies and gentlemen of their own opinions, that our coats might become an inch thickened with dust, before they would condescend to brush them; and our shoes might positively become *re-tanned* from constant wear, before they would clean them.   The *ladies* also partake the consequences of their mates, and it is with the greatest difficulty we can get our beds made, our rooms swept, or our china washed; it is all dirt, confusion, laziness, and insolence, from cook to cook's scullion, from commencement Tuesday to the tenth of October. You would be astonished at the airs these butterflies give themselves; they will not acknowledge a superior in the summer, though they live by and *out of* them: you shall see a fellow who, in term time, would do any dirty job with joy, and a hundred bows, in 'the long vacation' hold up his head as high as his betters, wear gloves upon his deep-grained hands, and have his fingers studded with rings; you shall see him either strutting up and down the streets, knocking his well-polished feet with a knowing cane, lounging at the college-gates, or stalking through the courts, as if he were a ' varment' character; or you shall see him mounted upon the best horse to be met with at the livery-stables, with boots and spurs, whip, and all the paraphernalia of an ' *eques ;*'—ogling all the women he meets with in his ride, or practising his *seatability* at a land-drain or bush-faggot; and only to be told by his position, by the inclination of his legs (which, like a pair of compasses, are generally stretched so as to form an angle of 90 degrees), by his holding by the saddle when the wind blows, for fear he should be unhorsed by the rude breath of Dan Boreas, from the master, whose horse he was formed to groom, rather than ride; whose boots he was intended to clean, rather than wear. I they meet you, they wont know you. If you want them to do an errand, they suit their own convenience. And this is Cambridge. But now, especially, are all sorts o people up in arms. The coaches are empty, and the drivers are longing for the beginning of term. The boat-keepers on the river are almost starved; and thei boats lie unused on the shore, except when some snob o other, equally as inexpert at the oar as the rein, takes shilling's worth of aquatics, at the risk of being run ove by a Littleport barge, or drowned in one of the locks. The gun-makers are glad to let their 'arms' to these asses also, who proceed in their master's jackets, if they happen to find the way to their wardrobes; poaching over all the manors in the neighbourhood, disturbing the game, and frightening the harvest-men, and giving, with all the nonchalence imaginable, the name and address o Mr. Such-an-one, of —— Col., or the Hon. G. So-and so, of —— Col., to the gamekeeper who is lucky enough to catch them."

"And this," thought I, "is the long vacation," as my friend ceased.—"Well, I have been for once taken in and, rather than let my friends know of my 'softness,' will be off as early to-morrow morning as possible." We exchanged a few more words of a consolatory nature, wishing him safe through all his troubles, and one of the "seventy;" and he wishing me, in a good glass of rea port (not à la Triston), a speedy and prosperous comple tion of my travels.

I slept very soundly at Mills's; and, after a hearty breakfast off *lime-scented* eggs, and *measured* bread and

Q

utter, at which my friend N—— joined me (though not
in the extravagant expense, which plainly showed I was
not out of Cambridge), I started next morning ; and, as
the Telegraph rolled along under the walls of the senate-
house, St. Mary's tolled the hour of nine. I cast a long
look, and sighed a *"vale iterumque vale,"* as the spires,
and steeples, and turrets of Granta vanished ; resolved
never again to visit college in " the long vacation," and
impressed with a worse opinion than ever of the spirit
which animates the town, and the folly which allows the
gown to be so imposed upon ; and cogitating deeply,
whether I had not at last found out the truth of the proverb, " experience is bought dear."—" Assuredly,"
thought I, " a little attention on the part of those who
should direct the affairs of this literary republic might
remedy some of its inconveniences, and, by so doing, re-
move the stigma which ever will attach to the education
of our youth, whilst suffered to be imposed upon and tre-
panned by creatures who are scarcely worthy to bear the
name of men.

Such was my reception at Cambridge during the long
vacation ; and such as it is I submit to the perusal of
your readers ; and I have no doubt they will find, that I
may put Q. E. D. at the foot of this paper without fear
of incurring the charge, " not proven." Should any of
them doubt my history, I would recommend them to
make a pilgrimage to the Cam, next autumn ; and, if
they do not quit it as speedily as I did, I will stake the
credit of a Jesuit, they are either radicals in principle, or
radically wrong in their affections, who feel invigorated
by the air which has so often vibrated with the shouts of
democracy, or who prefer solitude or a " den of thieves "
to the charms of society and the sweet interchange of

friendship from the hands of affection. I never knew any good of a man who stayed up during the summer; and I would, as an old friend to the gown, warn all enthusiastic Freshmen against such loss of time: it will assuredly end, from want of proper society, in a loss of morality, and, from want of a proper adjustment of pursuits, in the *wooden spoon* or an *apostleship;* but never in the way which alone can recompense them for the loss of friends, and the exclusion from all real comfort.

I send you this as one " gest" of my *voyages* in pursuit of experience ; and, hoping that you will regard the account as of indubitable origin, and the reflections arising therefrom, as partaking less of spleen than of goodwill towards all who may be in danger of a similar " take in," I freely subscribe the name which ought to bear respect from *all*, and the kind consideration, as a Dublin friend of mine would say, of *more!*

A Jesuit.

Davidson and Son,
Serle's Place, London.

This book should be returned to the Library on or before the last date stamped below.

A fine of five cents a day is incurred by retaining it beyond the specified time.

Please return promptly.

Check Out More Titles From HardPress Classics Series In this collection we are offering thousands of classic and hard to find books. This series spans a vast array of subjects — so you are bound to find something of interest to enjoy reading and learning about.

Subjects:
Architecture
Art
Biography & Autobiography
Body, Mind &Spirit
Children & Young Adult
Dramas
Education
Fiction
History
Language Arts & Disciplines
Law
Literary Collections
Music
Poetry
Psychology
Science
…and many more.

Visit us at www.hardpress.net